2/1

Also by John B. McGrath:

Watch This Movie
Cannes Confidential
New Zealand Love Story

IT'S ALL PART OF THE ALPINE EXPERIENCE

John B. McGrath

authorHOUSE®

AuthorHouse™ UK Ltd.
500 Avebury Boulevard
Central Milton Keynes, MK9 2BE
www.authorhouse.co.uk
Phone: 08001974150

First published by AuthorHouse   12/20/2010

ISBN: 978-1-4567-7101-0 (sc)
ISBN: 978-1-4567-7100-3 (hc)

To Ian, Catherine, Taylor and Rosie Smith

Acknowledgements

I am extremely grateful for the help I received in bringing this book to fruition, firstly, Sue Roberts who has been my sole confidant since I started writing and who has helped me immensely with editing. Kiki Carillon for introducing me to anyone and everyone in Chamonix and for damn fine dinner company. Michel Schruijer Gite le Belvédère, Martine Carrier Albert 1st, Russell Brice and Caroline Remond, Rob of Namaste Sports, Dave Elliot at The Office Bar, Mark Gear from All Mountain Performance, Ben and Emma from Le Marti, George Burdon of Dynamic Lives, Paul Holding and the Adventures of a Split-boarder, Mark Corville the world's oldest ski bum, Pistol Pete and Cecil, Jap John, Patrick Mackay, Doctor Aleid Ruijs, Dermott, Matt Whitaker, the Buff Boys Jules and Jimbo, Kenton Cool, Le Dahu Hotel, Le Vagabond, my brother Peter and sister-in-law Vikki and nieces Antonia and Helena for always having a welcoming home for me in Switzerland. Chamonix Tourism Office, Chamonix Mayor's office, Chamonix Alpine Museum. Also to the authors of some essential books I read such as: Mark Elling and The all Mountain Skier, Anne Sauvy Mountain Rescue Chamonix Mont Blanc, Robert MacFarlane Mountains of the Mind, Roland Huntford Two Planks and a Passion the dramatic history of skiing, Pierre Carrier and Peirre Maillet Stars & Mont Blanc and W. A. Bentley Snow Crystals.

Contents

Chapter One

An affair to remember - how I fell in love with snow skiing and all things Alpine

"Life is not about the number of breaths you take but by the number of moments that take your breath away."
Anon

I am standing at the entrance to the Vallée Blanche in the Chamonix Valley which is 3,842 meters above sea level. It's sometime in February 2010 which marks the middle of my ski season in Chamonix Mont Blanc. This is the highest altitude I have ever been to and even superior in height to the tallest peak in my native New Zealand, Mount Cook/Aoraki.

It has snowed ponderously for the last four days but has finally stopped and there are perfect crystal clear blue skies. As I struggle a little to acclimatise I am mesmerised by Europe's tallest peak, Mont Blanc, whose crown I think I could easily reach by teeing off with my One Wood - it seems that close up here on top of the European Alps.

I am fully equipped with ropes, crampons, avalanche transceiver, and probe and shovel as I will soon be skiing through a series of potentially deadly crevasses, glistening ice towers and beneath soaring seracs. As I am about to make my descent I am fully aware of how many people have lost their lives in this area and all of them with, I am sure, a similar expectation of the joy which is about to follow.

After walking through a longish ice tunnel and climbing down a retentive steep ridge I am ready to ski. I buckle in and point my fat long skis downhill and instantly I am skiing in knee deep fresh powder snow down an extraordinarily steep vertical drop. Suitable adjectives now seem impossible to describe the feeling I am having. It is a fully shaken not stirred cocktail of adrenalin, speed, fear and euphoria. I am as happy as I have ever been and feel completely free, content and intensely alive. Whatever this is, this feeling is the pre-eminent sensation in the world and my decision to spend a season in Chamonix Mont Blanc is summed up in these flawless minutes skiing in bottomless powder snow. I eventually need to stop for no other reason than to catch my breath and, of course, to look at my fresh lines like they are a piece of art as I selfishly admire my near perfect virgin tracks - like the whole world is watching and cares about nothing else. Yeah right!

I look around and I am feeling completely exhilarated by both the view of nothing but sky and ice and the inner buzz that this sort of unbelievable skiing creates. The Cheshire cat grin on my face is making me ache and is immovable. It is indeed hard to describe the feeling of skiing in fresh almost bottomless powder snow, but there is simply nothing that compares - it is just about you and the mountain and is uniquely personal.

"The sensual caress of waist deep cold smoke...glory in skiing virgin snow, in being the first to mark the powder with the signature of their run."
Tim Cahill

At intervals during what can be up to a 22km ski run (depending on the snow conditions) and is one of the world's longest routes, I watch other skiers and boarders tackle the same slopes, many with striking skill. I am envious watching them make first tracks until I am once again starting another adventure of my own navigating my way down one of the globe's most famous off piste ski slopes.

I am half way through my season in Chamonix and the skiing just gets better and better and better. Perhaps my confidence has grown in tackling many of the thousands of extreme ski runs Chamonix has had to offer me so far, or I have adjusted and have hardened up.

After being here a couple of months I fell in love with Chamonix but also was blown away by the people I met, the stories I heard, the history I learnt and what an unbelievable alpine experience this winter season was to offer me. Thus I felt completely inspired to write about my time here and you are reading the result.

Before I arrived in Chamonix, a few months previously, I had finished writing a screenplay set around skiing and a book which is my personal perspective of more than 1000 of my favourite movies - I have been a film critic for more than 15 years and wrote the book not only to help sell my screenplay but also to help hone my writing skills. Being something of a daydreamer I have found it hard throughout my life to control my hyper active energy, thoughts and creativity. I find writing just the ticket to perfectly balance my life and to give me a real sense of purpose that I have always longed for. We all go through different stages of life in our personal development and writing is, without doubt, that next stage for me.

In the process I fell deeply in love with writing so I decided to come to Chamonix Mont Blanc to be stimulated to write. I have always regarded Chamonix as the world's most famous ski resort and thus a perfect place to write and ski. By the end of this book you will be able to judge for yourself whether it merits that accolade.

This book is also a way of reminding me how lucky I am to have done the amount of skiing I have to date and to help me, and I hope you, appreciate the sport on a deeper level. Sometimes in life we get a little too complacent and take it for granted and I am an example of this.

I soon found that there was many a fine story to tell here, as well as introducing you to some of the astonishing people that were raised in the French Alps - locals or those that have been coming to Chamonix on a regular basis for many years - and that I was lucky enough to meet.

Over the winter season I met literally thousands of people through my work as a freelance chalet chef, through fellow chalet staff as well as in bars, restaurants and nightclubs not to mention on the ski fields, on chairlifts as well as on buses, trains and even hitch-hiking!

I also met numerous people at the seven different hotels, guest-houses and hostels I called home during my stay - especially Gite le Belvédère where I spent 50 nights.

It meant I talked to seasonaires, recreational skiers, snow boarders, ski tourers, ski bums, hotel management, corporate groups, family groups, guys on stag parties, extreme and free skiers, ski racers, children, students studying French, post graduates having a season out before they enter the workforce, the unemployed or those that had lost their jobs, strippers, gamblers, gigolos, professional skiers and boarders, authors and writers, poets, journalists, artists, the local Gendarmes, doctors, nurses, mountain rescue personnel, helicopter pilots, museum staff, historians, photographers, para-gliders, ice climbers, rock climbers, mountain climbers, entertainers, musicians, cross country skiers, ice hockey players, snow walkers, tourists, sight seers, retailers, wine merchants, food wholesalers, film makers, photographers, ski instructors, mountain guides, pisters and Compagnie du Mont Blanc staff!

Those I did not meet by chance, but thought essential to interview in order to tell a more thorough Chamonix story, I arranged to meet: including the Chamonix tourism office; the local Mayor's office; prominent alpine guides; ski instructors; extreme skiers and professional skiers; restaurant and bar owners and a myriad of those I found remotely interesting.

I found an accumulation of information about Chamonix and many books that have already been written about either the skiing or climbing here. For instance Chamonix is the oldest ski resort in France and is the third most visited natural site in the world and has more than five million visitors per year. But, I wanted to find out the pulse of what made the town pump and learn why Chamonix is called the most famous ski and alpine resort in the world and to write a book that presented a rationale for such a prestigious title. Through my own experiences I wanted to discover for myself whether it deserved such an esteemed claim to international fame.

After some solid research I soon found there was plenty to read about the area and an abundance of fascinating stories about the people who made it so famous and why. I discovered many books on Chamonix, which I read during the season and which I mention and also take quotes from. A great deal of the books I read were historic, alpine related and stories of many of the famous guides or climbers who added to the fame and glory of the region. Every book I read I really enjoyed and found both inspiring and fascinating but it soon became clear there was nothing like what I wanted to attempt to write. So I made up my mind there was nothing like experiencing it yourself and there was also nothing like meeting the current legends who would become the future's history.

There is so much more to skiing and the overall alpine experience that only skiing can give you than meets the eye and very few books are available which talk much about it apart from conspicuously commercial titles, personal memoirs written by acknowledged experts and personalities together with the odd ski guide or instructors manual. They all have their uses but I wanted to delve into the philosophy and psychology of skiing and of alpinism and also what motivation makes some humans pushing their death barrier limits every day. I wanted to look at the equilibrium of risk and pleasure and relate it not only to skiing but also to personal development and point out such obvious comparisons. And I just happened to end up in the most perfect place on earth to write just such a book - Chamonix Mont Blanc the birthplace of alpinism and of extreme skiing!

I also wanted to write about all the other ingredients that complete the alpine experience such as mountaineering, alpine food and wine, the chalet business, the social scene, the local scene and interesting people I met along the way. I also believe there is not a ski resort in the world that could provide better fodder for this type of book.

With the utmost confidence and a wry smile, I must also add that I am downright qualified to write such a book as I have tried almost all of the bang-up adrenalin fixes life has to offer.

Firstly I have not missed a ski season since I first hit the slopes in 1976. I was in a ski race team for both the local province and my school. I have introduced hundreds of people to the sport and have passed my New Zealand Certificate in Ski Instructing. I have raced the masters on a regular basis and speed skied to 153km and whenever anyone has ever asked me what I do or like, skiing is always and has always been at the forefront.

I have also climbed mountains, sky dived, deep water dived, water skied at over 100 km per hour, wind surfed, white water rafted, white water kayaked and sailed on Maxis and super-yachts. I have competed in triathlons, all day mountain multi-sport events and marathons. I have been under the card in golf dozens of times, I have show jumped and evented horses, driven super fast cars around race circuits and owned cross county motor bikes as well as plenty of fast cars.

It can also be said that I have spent many years wasting my life away in nightclubs getting my fix on as much sex, drugs and rock and roll as possible. There are many other things I have tried once or twice as well but none I have to say, comparable to the completeness of skiing.

So first let me give you a little background on myself in regards to skiing. I was first introduced to it in 1976 when our family shifted from the Solomon Islands to live in the New Zealand Alps. We lived in a beautiful small high country town called Twizel that had sensational views of the surrounding Alps including New Zealand's highest peak Mount Cook - since renamed Mount Aoraki. In many ways the area has a lot in common with Chamonix but on a much less populated basis. Many New Zealand guides have started their climbing careers there and have subsequently moved to Chamonix to work and live.

In my teens I became obsessed with skiing and was soon working on the lifts and in ski hire at Lake Ohau my local ski-field which was only half an hour's drive away. It was privately owned with the longest T-bar in the country and a small Pomer lift on the beginners' slope. It still very much maintains a club like atmosphere and to this day is known as one of New Zealand's friendliest ski-fields. I was as happy as Larry working there and spent many hours listening to stories from the European, Canadian and American ski instructors and ski patrol of their alpine adventures. It instilled in me a spirit of adventure for "more" that has never left.

This is when I first learnt about Chamonix and of course Mont Blanc. When I left school I was determined to have a full winter season in Europe working for a ski school in the Swiss Alps but it was not to be. In 1991, I was moving to Japan to work on a ski-field but stopped off in Sydney, and ended up staying four years and had very little skiing during that time. I left Sydney to move to Aspen Colorado but stopped off in New Zealand and ended up staying there 15 years; admittedly I did have four full seasons in that time and easily warranted my season pass every other year.

Even though I have skied various resorts in France, Switzerland, Italy and Austria I have never had more than a few weeks at a time and by no means a complete European alpine experience.

Well after all these years later, circumstances have prevailed and I find myself having the full ski season I have only ever dreamed of and in a resort that makes, and has always made, every top ten ski resort list in the world.

"The ski bum trades security for face shots, the future for the moment. Considering how hollow the promise of a corporate career has become, who can say the ski bum is not the wiser investor in his or her youth."
Anon

Like many people that are attracted to the Alps to live, work or play, to escape or forget, I guess this is also the story of a 46 year old having a mid life quandary and how the mountains can liberate and disentangle you no matter how much pain you are carrying or what burden you bare. I am living proof of that.

"Forty is the old age of youth. Fifty is the youth of old age"
Victor Hugo

Chamonix was to present me with the perfect opportunity to mull over things that have happened to me and lay them to eternal rest. For reasons I will reveal I was carrying emotional baggage, guilt, fears, and resentments that needed to be worked through and left behind once and for all. I am sure you can get rid of your baggage anywhere no matter what form it comes in but the Alps just happened to be the perfect place for me. As I discovered over the season I certainly wasn't alone as I was to meet dozens of people in a similar boat and which indeed confirmed I had come to the perfect place.

I have filled the book with many of my favourite quotes that are both motivational and inspirational to help get my message across and that relate to that particular topic or chapter. Some were found while I was reading everything I could about Chamonix's history. Some of the quotes are from the very best in their field should it be free skiing, extreme skiing, competitive skiing, mountaineering, climbing or the appreciation of food and wine.

***"The tragedy of life is in what dies inside a man while he lives
– the death of genuine feeling, the death of inspired response,
the awareness that makes it possible to feel the pain or the
glory of other men in yourself."***
Norman Cousins

Equally as important is that this is a story of one of the last frontiers of off piste skiing, the wild west of skiing if you like, and now named by many as the death sport capital of the world; Chamonix Mont Blanc. It is only a matter of time before off piste skiing is strictly controlled, administered and regulated to ensure safety; although I agree with these regulations being enforced in the future it will diminish a certain amount of freedom that we now enjoy.

The book also draws comparisons with many of the other internationally acclaimed European ski resorts that I have visited, to demonstrate that I am in no way biased towards Chamonix. For instance I compare facilities, skiable terrain and resort hospitality.

This is also a personal perspective based on my experiences, research, reading, films, skiing and meetings with many of the living legends in Chamonix; it is in no way meant to be a definitive guide, simply something I would have liked to have read before I arrived here. My one and only wish is that the ski bug and magic of the alpine experience I have been infected with for 35 years rubs off on you and you too get hooked or rediscover a lost passion.

"The essence of life is finding something you really love and then making the daily experience worthwhile."
Denis Waitley

Chapter Two
Why I ended up in Chamonix

"The refusal to rest content, the willingness to risk excess on behalf of one's obsessions, is what distinguishes artists from entertainers, and what makes some artists adventurers on behalf of us all.
John Updike

How does a single 46 year old single male end up having a full winter season by himself in one of the world's premier ski resorts, is probably a very good question, so let me start with my background.

I have been mainly self-employed in the last 25 years and I will not bore you with too many details but I have owned a ski and surf shop, a horse riding school, an event management company as well as owning or co-owning a swag of restaurants, cafés and bars. I have also worked in the corporate world in merchant banking, insurance and finance. I get bored easily and I have always found business initially exciting but eventually lose interest and that's the reason why I have never really stuck to anything business wise for very long. I have never been bored skiing!

Before arriving in Chamonix I was still getting over failed relationships and a restaurant business not working out - I had lost focus, passion and interest in my businesses and in life so I would spend most of my time either in the cinema or on the ski field where I am always my happiest. I had been writing what I would call seriously for three years and having completed my book **"Watch This Movie"** and screenplay **"New Zealand Love Story"** I was perhaps a little over confident as I thought they would both be an instant success and become very profitable overnight. It was not quite the case but writing them has certainly opened up a whole new world to me and it's why I came to Chamonix.

My plan was to travel to the Venice Film Festival, then the Zurich Film Festival and finally to the world's largest book fair in Frankfurt to sell my book and screenplay then go home and pay off my debts. To cut a long story short, my 600 page book needed some serious editing which I did not have the income to provide and I refused to sell it to a remorseless publisher. My screenplay needed more work but at around 30 million US$ was mostly just too expensive to make for a first feature.

Some good doctor friends of mine were at the Frankfurt book fair. They had set up a brilliant company publishing children's medical comics explaining illness in terms children can understand called Medikidz. The next thing I knew I was working for them in their plush offices in Chelsea and living in South Kensington, London.

It was, however, starting to get very cold and my thoughts quickly turned to the slopes - they do every year when ever winter starts as I have this uncontrollable urge to go skiing. I began spending plenty of time in the ski shop down on the Kings Road and bought every ski magazine that was available. Even though the long term prospects of working for my doctor friends were very good I realised the corporate world was no longer me. So I had my first real opportunity of having a full season living and working somewhere in the European Alps, it was a tantalising prospect.

About five years previously I had passed the current ski instructors exams in New Zealand, so I started applying for instructing jobs around Europe. I had been a guest at one of my friend's wedding in St Moritz in the summer and I fell in love with the place – I got to the top of every peak that was open. However, I was put off by how expensive everything was and after a few nights out socialising, and watching the rich and famous play, I decided I did not have the income to warrant such a lavish existence. If I had I would have been cocooned in someone else's bubble and that form of shallow state no longer attracted me.

It's fine sitting around a table drinking copious amounts of Vintage Krug or Crystal after skiing until it is your turn to pay the bill. There were so many jowly bordering on obese older, obviously very rich men with stunning young girlfriends, it either made me sick or entirely jealous. Many of them were Russian whose new found richness dominates many of the chic alpine resorts, whatever it was as much as there was a certain attraction it was not my scene and looking back I would have got bored with the skiing. If not bored, my skiing would never have progressed at the rate it did in Chamonix. I certainly wouldn't have written this particular book. There are certainly many ski resorts in Europe that are better known for the jet-set crowd they attract and what goes on socially more than for the seriousness of all things alpine.

My heart was set on getting a job in one of Europe's top five resorts so my other main consideration was St Anton in Austria. I had skied before and had an awesome time both on the slopes and après but I could not find a suitable job there at the beginning of the season.

There are numerous ski job websites where you can place your CV and wait hopefully for someone to contact you such as skijobs.co.uk or natives. co.uk. and hundreds of ski resorts in Europe, Japan, Canada and the USA with thousands of job vacancies for a zillion types of jobs but majority in hospitality.

Initially I was contacted by several Japanese ski resorts but I left them at bay in hope of a better offer coming in. I was surprised that there was quite a lot of interest in me and I put that down to my age as the majority of other ski instructors applying for jobs would be half my age.

I was then contacted by a fellow New Zealander who was CEO of a business called Dynamic Lives based in Chamonix. He arranged to meet me in a trendy bar/restaurant in Notting Hill called the Eclectic. I went along to the interview with George who gave me an irksome spiel about his luxury chalet company - which was a little unusual especially as I thought I was applying for a ski instructing job. It soon became clear the position he was interviewing me for was as a chef; he had read on my resume that I had owned or co-owned a bunch of restaurants, bars and cafés and that I am a passionate and experienced cook – all very true.

George was also pretty damn good at talking, convincingly so, and by the time he finally stopped I was pretty convinced that Chamonix sounded as astounding as I had heard and was somewhere I would fit right in – oh, and the skiing he mentioned sounded unreal. He also convinced me that there would be plenty of time to ski as the chef job he was offering was on a freelance basis but with the guarantee of seven weeks work during the season.

The job offer was ideal as the money when I worked was excellent; it would allow plenty of time to ski and also enough time to work on my screenplay and novel. I also mentioned that I was a qualified ski instructor and he said if the opportunity arose I would be able to teach the clients if they did not want to use the local instructors. So I said sure to all his eventual questions and the next thing I knew, I had accepted the job.

I thought I had better brush up my best chef skills, especially as the cooking I would be doing was for the very high end of the luxury market. The only condition was that I had to buy my own car and George suggested it would be cheaper to buy a car in London and drive it across France to Chamonix. After searching on the net for a week or two, I eventually found a 1995 Chrysler Jeep owned by a cow farmer about 20km outside Brighton.

I packed my bags and left the exciting international metropolis of London and arrived in Brighton to pick up my Jeep which I named Charlie (there was an old horse staring at me in the next paddock which reminded me of one in a book I read as a child called Old Charlie).

Charlie had been sitting outside for what looked like the last decade. He was midnight blue and had black tinted windows – and was growing moss all over. But I was happy as I thought he was the world's best bargain for £370. It was obviously a little bit of a risk driving such a car most of the way across France but what the hell I thought, let's throw caution into the wind.

> *"As you grow older, you'll find the only things you regret are the things you didn't do."*
> **Zachary Scott**

I had driven across France from London once before along the motorways to Cannes and found it exceedingly monotonous so I decided to make the journey as exceptionally scenic and enjoyable as possible so I researched the most scenic route and this is what I came up with.

I took the ferry from Dover to Dunkirk and then drove through St Omer, Lillers, Bethune, Lens, Dougal, Cambrai, St Quentin, Laon, Reims, Troyes, Chatillion, Dijon, Beaune, Chalon, Tournus, Bourg, Nantua, Bellegrade, Annemasse, Cluses, Sallanche and finally to Chamonix. I mention the route as the drive is superb as you pass through all of these towns and cities many of which are historic. The other benefit is that you never have to venture onto the motor way which means you will not have to pay any road tolls. My advice would be only ever taking the motorway if you are in a rush.

The highlights for me were definitely the Champagne and Burgundy regions where I stayed and enjoyed several wine tastings. You obviously need more time than a night in these towns but I had visited both areas before in the summer with much joy and wonderful memories.

I have travelled to close on 50 countries and driven across a lot of Europe, Asia, coast to coast in America, half of Australia and all of New Zealand many times but nothing really compares to France. I am not saying France is superior to the others but it's unique and of course very French as one would hope. You only appreciate how very rural a country it is when you drive across it. Long timeless colour changing agricultural plains, charming authentic villages, miles and miles of vineyards, rich lush forests, rolling green hills and meandering rivers and vibrant historic cities such as Lyon. And then you enter the Alps and the whole country takes on another dimension and you discover some of the most beautiful alpine scenery to be found anywhere on the planet.

Driving across a country gives you a realistic feel for its size and geography that cannot be compared to when you take public transport. You stop when you want to, sleep when you chose and take whatever route tickles your fancy. There are umpteen first-class books on this route but my advice is drive it in the summer as the beginning of winter is very bleak and you often have the worst weather of the year - it poured with rain for the first day and a half of my journey before becoming very overcast and freezing when I got out of the car!

There has, and will always be, something magical about driving a long distance with the growing anticipation that your destination is just going to be awesome. When there is a positive expectancy and hope, how can one possibly not be happy?

In my youth the ski-fields were at my doorstep, which I would somewhat take for granted, that is until I had to move to the big city for work. But once you have given your heart to the mountains it never changes no matter how much travelling you do, or what other pursuits you get caught up in. The mountains always draw you back like a magnet to where you belong. There is something profoundly and overwhelmingly satisfying knowing that whatever happens in life you will always find an incessant happiness and contentment in the Alps.

"The use of travelling is to regulate imagination by reality, and instead of thinking how things may be, to see them as they are."
Samuel Johnson

Dynamic Lives prided themselves about being a luxury travel experience and chalet company so I had put together a vast collection of upmarket alpine recipes I had printed out from the internet as well as a collection of recipes from the restaurants I had been involved in. I had thousands of thoughts about what seemed to me to be every dish I had either cooked, seen cooked or eaten as I tried to reassure myself that cooking in this upmarket environment was going to be a breeze.

It never ceases to amaze me what one's memory can recall when you really put your mind to it - especially with taste. I often pulled over and scribbled down another dish I had recollected that I thought would go down well in the Alps. I had always thought there were two types of people in this world, those who could cook and those who couldn't and I was certainly one who could. How many times have you been to a restaurant and been totally disappointed in the food knowing you could easily cook the dish way better?

Another benefit about Chamonix was the local cinema multiplex that shows all the latest films in English. The latest movies are something I cannot live without and something you will not find in many other resorts. I doubt whether there would be anyone else with a similar motivation.

I was totally hyped about the up and coming season especially as Chamonix was always a ski resort that was consistently mentioned and recommended by other skiers I had met throughout my years of skiing, but mostly what excited me was that I was finally going to have a full season in the European Alps in what I had always regarded as one of the best resorts. As the town is also just as famous for its climbing I was excited that I would soon be living in an environment which is rich in history not just for skiing but also all things alpine. It's funny how often you initially associate a place with a name, a reputation and the people instead of the landscape you are expecting.

*"Chamonix is the birthplace of Alpinism. It's the motherland.
In the seventies and eighties it was held up as this larger
than life destination, oh Cham, Cham on ix, it was almost
mythical. You would aspire to go and ski Chamonix."*
Steve Casimiro, Powder Magazine - STEEP

Chapter Three

Chamonix Mont Blanc the birthplace and world capital of alpinism and extreme skiing

"It looks like a city of obelisks, columns and pyramids, a city of temples and sepulchres: a palace built by fairies for disembodied spirits."
Victor Hugo

It was a dazzling, effervescent, crisp, clean day when I first laid my eyes on Mont Blanc; perfect clear blue skies and the mountain seems to come out of nowhere and from 1000 metres up and up it goes to its peak 4,810 meters. The road reminded me of the yellow brick road in "The Wizard of Oz" as it curves and winds its way through a series of long steep gullies and aspiring mountains to the bottom of Mont Blanc.

The colossal alabastrine glaciers and cold blue spires looked like they could easily tumble on top of you as you drive into the town centre. My smile beamed as Charlie and I drove into Chamonix with the shining white towers glowingly welcoming us.

"The doors to this mythical garden will open before you."
Gaston Rebuffat

It was Friday December the 11th and after trying for a few days, I still hadn't connected with George despite having left a ton of messages. Chamonix was not what I had expected and I guess I was thinking it would look more like the other European resorts I had visited. The reason being, Chamonix is not just a ski resort - it is a mountain town which is even busier in the summer. The resort is very similar to Banff in Canada. It is also not a ski-in ski-out resort like many of the others. It has a population of close to 10,000 and that climbs to over 100,000 daily in the winter and over 130,000 in the summer.

I parked the car next to the local Olympic size ice skating rink where the Chamonix ice hockey team usually sell out every time they play. I had arrived at lunch time and was a little anxious as George had still not picked up the phone. However, it gave me to the opportunity to sight-see firsthand. I had read as much as I could find online about Chamonix but don't you find that when you actually get to a destination that what you had imagined is completely different.

I found a busy pizza restaurant in the middle of town with plenty of people sitting outside and sat down with a large beer and enjoyed my first taste of Chamonix hospitality as I split my time between people and Alp gazing. It was bloody freezing and all the passers-by were dressed in their winter woollies and so were their dogs!

I enjoy walking and exploring any new destination for the first time and there was plenty to see. I soon found the famous gondola and cable car that both leave from different spots in Chamonix. One is the legendary Aiguille du Midi which is the highest cable car in Europe and where you can ski 22km down the world famous Vallée Blanche. The other is the Planpraz bubble that takes you to the up to the Brevant ski-field. I wanted to get on immediately and get to the top and get some turns in.

Even though Chamonix is not a ski-in ski-out resort the surrounding mountains are as spectacular as you will see anywhere in the world and you are absorbed in the natural elevation and peaks just by walking about. As I was wandering around gazing at the Alps I slipped on some ice, went airborne and fell right onto the middle of my back. I seriously thought I had broken something as a couple of non-English speaking passers-by helped me up. An older woman and her very pretty daughter were saying all sorts of things to me in French suggesting, I presume, that visiting the local hospital might be a good idea. I thanked them for their concern and staggered off to buy myself a stiff drink and to gauge any potential damage.

Christ, imagine coming all this way and not even making it to the slopes as I staggered off in intense pain. I popped into the Bar des Sports which a famous bar in the middle of town which guides and ski instructors have been frequenting for years. I rested my back as I enjoyed a single malt which I thought was quite good value for six Euros.

"Every sport has its Mecca. Free climbers to Yosemite, mountain bikers to Lake Garda, white water paddlers to Voss and extreme skiers to Chamonix."
Kayak Magazine

It was pleasing to see that Chamonix has all the advantages of a town. Plenty of choice of retail outlets, boutique shops including a reasonable supermarket as well as an abundance of bars and restaurants - something I am always most interested in seeing. I unwaveringly believe that the hospitality of a town or resort is reflected in the service it provides to its visitors and so far I was impressed as there was plenty of everything to suit all ages, budgets and pallets.

The very centre of Chamonix is pedestrianised which makes it very user friendly and gives it a busy alpine village type atmosphere especially with the vista of the surround Alps. By walking through the streets and popping in and out of shops, restaurants and bars I soon got a feel of it and I found it to be richly cosmopolitan and vibrant.

If you are not exactly familiar with the area Chamonix is snuggled into the heart of the northern Alps at the intersection of the three borders separating France, Italy and Switzerland. The motorway network that serves the region terminates at the entrance to the valley with the Auto Route Blanche E25-A40. Hence, Chamonix is surprisingly close to major European towns and international airports, in particular Geneva, Lyon and Turin (via the Mont Blanc tunnel).

As Geneva is just under a two hour flight from London, Chamonix, as you can imagine, is very popular with the Brits and many fly over for a weekend's skiing. You can also get there by rail with a connection either at St Gervais, where you can connect to any major city in France, or Vallorcine where you can connect to anywhere in Switzerland.

There is without a doubt a Swiss and Italian influence in the town due to this proximity of the borders and this is heavily reflected in the architecture, food, wine and what I gather of the culture so far. I am later told by the tourism office that no other resort in the world offers such a diverse range of attractions and gauging by the amount of brochures, flyers and point of sale I see they do have an excellent point - there is a huge array of options about how to spend your time there.

The tourism office helped me with the following information so I will also add a little geography which will help paint the bigger picture and will also help later on when I am explaining places I have visited.

The region is called the Arve valley, Haute-Savoie, France. Chamonix is situated in the north-western part of the Alps, just 15 km away from the Swiss border via the Col des Montets and 15km from Italy via the Mont Blanc tunnel. The converging point of these three countries is the summit of Mont Dolent (3820m). Of glacial origin, the valley is dominated by the Mont Blanc massif to the south and the Aiguilles Rouges mountains to the north. It extends over 17 km from the top of the Col de Montets to the Taconnaz torrent covering a surface area of 24,546 hectares. There are 38,000 hectares of nature reserve and 18,000 hectares of classified site. The centre of Chamonix is located at an altitude of 1,035 m and the highest village in the valley is Le Tour at 1,462 m.

Chamonix is twinned with Aspen (USA), Davos (Switzerland), Fujioshida (Japan), Garmisch-Partenkirchen (Germany) and Courmayeur (Italy). People come from all four corners of the world to visit. I find myself in the company of people from every country you can imagine, mutually fuelled by a passion for some of the world's best off piste skiing as Chamonix attracts mainly expert skiers who want to test their skills in the off piste terrain.

Chamonix became famous internationally in 1924 when it hosted the very first Winter Olympics - even though it was celebrated for alpinism and luxury alpine holidays many years before that. Chamonix has always been ranked as one of the top ten ski resorts in the world and also ranks among the elite of contenders for the title of the world's most famous ski resort. My research for this book indicates it is the world's most famous resort because it is an all-year-round destination, attracts the high tourist numbers with the widest range of activities to offer. Most people do not come to Chamonix for the ritz or glitz that many of the other contenders offer but for the challenge of testing themselves against Europe's most spectacular slopes.

I love statistics so let me tell you which of the globe's other top ski resorts form the top ten as voted by The Travellers' Digest. It's totally consistent with almost any other top ten list you can find anywhere. This list has been consistent for more than 50 years with the exception of the addition of

Whistler which opened in 1966. The list was put together through readership ratings, reviews and popularity. The resorts are judged for the quality of snow, elevation, skiable terrain, village atmosphere, transport, retail, après skiing, options for dining and drinking, accommodation choice and other snow related activities. They are also in order from number one to number ten. However I do not completely agree with the list and have put together my own top ten next to it.

	Traveller's Digest	John McGrath
1.	Whistler Black-Comb, Canada	Chamonix, Mont Blanc
2.	Kitzbuhel, Austria	St Anton, Austria
3.	Zermatt, Switzerland	Whistler Black-Comb, Canada
4.	Vail, Colorado	Vail Colorado
5.	Banff Lake Louise, Alberta, Canada	Banff Lake Louise, Alberta Canada
6.	Chamonix Mont Blanc	Kitzbuhel, Austria
7.	Stowe, Vermont, USA	Verbier, Switzerland
8.	Mont-Tremblant, Quebec, Canada	Val d'Isere, France
9.	Cortina, Italy	Aspen, Colorado
10.	Aspen, Colorado	Cortina, Italy

I have taken out Zermatt as even though it has a wonderful traffic-free village atmosphere and stunning views of the Matterhorn, the skiing does not compete with the other resorts. Stowe because the weather is shockingly cold and its small slopes and Monte-Tremblant for no other reason than it got axed by the competition. I have added St Anton, Verbier and Val d'Isere for all the reasons I mentioned above. All three of these resorts have also undergone some major development and increased facilities and are all mammoth in size. Chamonix of course makes it to the number one slot for all the reason I mention in this book.

It is also interesting that Chamonix is one of the ten most expensive ski resorts in Europe. This is calculated on property prices, accommodation, transport, lift passes, ski lessons, eating out, the average price for a pint of beer, cup of coffee, etc. The ten most expensive ski resorts in Europe are:

1. Courchevel, France
2. Meribel, France
3. St Moritz, Switzerland
4. Val d'Isere, France

5. Zermatt, Switzerland
6. Verbier, Switzerland
7. Kitzbuhel, Austria
8. Megeve, France
9. Villars, Switzerland
10. Chamonix, France

You might be surprised that resorts like Gstaad in Switzerland - which boasts three five star hotels - and Klosters in Switzerland don't make the top ten, and that France has half of the top ten. The reason for that is that France is immensely influenced by the British pound due to its proximity and no other country in the world offers as much ski- in ski-out accommodation so it quite simply becomes a question of supply and demand.

Of Chamonix's foreign visitors in the winter: 55% are from Great Britain, 12% from Sweden, 7% from Russia, 3% from the USA and then 2% from each of Italy, Switzerland, Spain and Belgium. There are a bunch of other countries on 1% such as The Netherlands, Norway and Germany with the statistics changing dramatically in the summer.

Back at the Bar de Sports, while more single malt was working its magic and healing my painful back, I had picked up a local magazine and a local female author had said Chamonix is about radical challenge, extreme and crazy performance and attracts people with a taste for the inaccessible which is genetic in the valley.

I looked around the Bar des Sports, which has large carvings of historic mountaineering feats as well as a variety of rugged looking mountain types, it was easy to make quick assessments of what she was talking about as my mind was overexcited about my first day's skiing.

> **"Security is mostly a superstition. It does not exist in nature**
> **or the children of men as a whole experience it. Avoiding**
> **danger is no safer in the long run than outright exposure.**
> **Life is either a daring adventure or nothing."**
> **Helen Keller 1880 – 1968**

With much relief I finally got hold of George and we met for a beer at The Mix Bar (a small somewhat trendy upmarket bar catering for the more discerning 30 to 50 year old). It was perfectly located on the Arve River which gracefully travels through the middle of town.

George and his business partner (who I never met) had managed and owned Dynamic Lives for ten years. It was a successful chalet and event business that had grown steadily and had peaked a few years ago when the economy was booming, especially in the area of corporate events. Then the recession came and with it a mammoth downward spiral that kicked the living day lights out of both the luxury chalet business and corporate events in particular. In the summer Dynamic Lives was even busier renting and managing villas in Ibiza.

Many similar companies folded, but George persevered and restructured and the business is now starting to pick up again. Even though he never took me up on my many offers to interview him I found it admirable that: firstly he had given up a successful corporate life to live in the Alps or as he put it: **"It's a lifestyle choice not a financial one"**; secondly for his family background. George was born and raised on a family farm just outside Queenstown, New Zealand where he attended the very best private schools and was a competent skier in his youth.

The reason I mention this is the Otago High Country is some of the most beautiful in the world and the inspiration for two screenplays of mine. His decision to live in the French Alps was one I found intriguing and inspiring and helped confirm to me that I was in the right resort for the winter for sure.

After a few cold beers we then drove up to Argentiere which is a historic village 10 minutes drive from Chamonix. Argentiere is at over 1200 metres altitude and like many old alpine villages remains authentic retaining a timeless alpine charm and is quite unlike Chamonix. We drove in the snow through the oldest part of the village, past the old Baroque church and snow covered graveyard to La Ferme de Varaita which is one of the luxury chalets that Dynamic Lives rent during the season. George and his wife were staying there while their own house was being renovated. My greeting was quite memorable as George's wife made it quite clear she had only cooked for two and I was not really welcome.

Well as you can imagine after driving for four and a half days and walking around Chamonix most of the day I was a little pissed off and a little pissed as I had been drinking for most of the afternoon. Oh well I thought, it gave me another opportunity to have a look around. I wandered through Argentiere and was very taken with the village layout, senescent streets, the ancient graveyard next to a charming octogenarian church, rattling old stone buildings and aged wooden chalets that were almost completely covered in snow all surrounded by snow clad pine trees. The narrow main street was full of little ski and retail shops, restaurants and bars, the odd hotel and Christmas lights were beaming everywhere the eye could see. It was picture postcard perfect. The valley's religious architectural heritage is particularly interesting as I was to discover numerous chapels, churches, crosses and shrines that bear witness to the customs and traditions of past times.

Argentiere was very quiet, still almost like being on the ocean when it is dead calm, and then I remembered I had become a Facebook fan of Chamonix's leading night club No-Escape. It just happened to be having its winter season opening night, tonight, so I drove back down the hill into Chamonix town to check it out.

For 10.00pm on a Friday night it was altogether pulse-less as was the grand opening of No-Escape. The venue was very cool, modern, hip and as stylish as any top club you would find anywhere in Europe- all it lacked this night was enough people. I soon found out that it doubled for a strip bar called Seventh Heaven. We all have our flaws and I guess table dancing bars would have to be one of mine in the past.

I had a couple more drinks and soon got talking to a few of the girls who looked completely bored and it was easy to tell that they were thinking that spending a season in Chamonix stripping was perhaps not the best financial decision they had ever made. I tried to convince them otherwise and also suggested that I would be more than keen to help improve their skiing by offering them free ski lessons for lap dances! I also offered to show them my lap dancing skills which I must say they were quite taken with. I realised I was by now well under the weather and that driving back up to Argentiere drunk was perhaps not very wise. Imagine spending your first night in a French jail locked up for drunk driving and perhaps sharing the cell with a few of the local drunks or other depressed ski bums and then being booted out of town like the star of one of those old western movies.

Definitely not a cracking way to start the ski season so being as sensible as I could, I said goodbye to my new Eastern European stripper friends and went for a wander. I could not find people anywhere and perhaps that was due to the fact that it was remorselessly freezing. It was also the very beginning of the season. I felt like I was in the blasted Antarctic not in the French Alps. Each time I breathed in it felt like someone was blowing dry ice down my throat with the power of a raging fire extinguisher that reverberated with every breath.

As I did not know my around yet I was to find out later that you do need to know where to go to find the masses on any given night as there is always a busy bar in Chamonix during the winter season. I sobered up in what seemed like minutes and ventured back to Charlie who was frozen over and I could not open the damned door. After about 10 minutes without gloves (or hat) I finally managed to open the door after a lot of banging kicking and cursing. This unfortunately was to happen again and again when the temperatures dropped which I can assure you is a real pain in the arse when you have to drive 8km on frozen roads to cook breakfast for waiting guests at 6.30am in the morning.

My hands felt like they had frost bite and my teeth were chattering and I was sure I had never been this cold before. By the time Charlie's heater was working I was back in Argentiere where, back at the chalet, I cranked up the heater in my room to full and slept like a log and dreamt of all things white and big mountain skiing.

"Chamonix is one of those places in the world of skiing that every time you go there, there's some chance that you will leave in a body-bag, so this makes it a higher intensity spot than most places that you go to. It's the place, you are not a big mountain skier until you have skied Chamonix."
Tim Petrick, K2 Sports

Chapter Four
The Chamonix Chalet Business

"It is only in adventure that some people succeed in knowing themselves – in finding themselves."
Andre Gide 1869 – 1951

The majority of tourists that visit Chamonix stay in hotels, rent apartments or stay in a chalet. I think a chalet stay offers the advantages of making the most of and quite often determine the success of your alpine experience. The chalet business in Chamonix is world renown and thus I thought is important to write about earlier on in this piece.

My first day's mission was to find somewhere to live as I was going to start work the next day cooking with another chef in a very upmarket chalet called Le Marti. The view from the chalet was sensational vistas of the Grand Montets ski-field and the surrounding Alps. You could see people skiing in the far distance like ants on sugar which excited me to no end.

George's wife did not realise I was the new chef and apologised for her previous greeting. She thought George had just brought a stray home from the pub to justify his lateness. She also gave me a wonderful introduction to Chamonix, her time there and how she had met George at the Clubhouse where she had worked with a mutual friend of ours a few years back.

It had snowed overnight and I had not bought snow tyres for Charlie yet. In France you must have snow tyres or carry chains even if your car is a four wheel drive, in many countries like Switzerland snow tyres are compulsory. I had neither and George took one look at Charlie, the amount of snow, the growing moss, smiled and said: "Well John it's all part of the alpine experience." And that's how I came up with the title for this book. Charlie ploughed through the fresh snow easily and off I went to check out the Saturday market and en route I hoped to find somewhere to live.

The traditional Saturday market is held in the large open local square in Chamonix which has impressive views of the surrounding Alps including Mont Blanc. It is active with a variety of topical stalls featuring cured meats, fresh fish, butchery, bakery, cheeses, fruit and vegetables, chutneys, pickles and jams, dried fruit and nuts as well as clothing, ski wear and household goods. It was also a swell place to have lunch as there was a solid variety of stalls selling hot crepes, mulled wine, aperitifs, baguettes etc. There were also some excellent Italian stalls with cured meats, pastas and aged parmigiana. You could also buy local Foie Gras, truffles, duck and wild game.

In the early days of mountain rescue there was no permanent shelter for the rescue helicopter so they parked it in the market square too. On one occasion when the pilot came to pick it up he found it being used to hold bags of fruits and the like - just imagine if there was an urgent rescue! The market was also very communal and obviously a weekly meeting place for the locals to catch up with each other. I loved it and went back on a regular basis over the entire season and got to know many of the locals on a first name basis.

The temperature was well in the minuses and I was intensely cold so I stocked up on some new winter gloves and hat which were an absolute bargain. As with any other French towns the customary markets are indicative of the fresh and local produce that is readily available. The markets are also so distinctively French that you know you could be nowhere else.

I then ventured off to find somewhere to live. George had indicated that it would be a breeze finding accommodation but after a week or two of looking I found this not to be the case so I ended up staying in cheap hotels, guest-houses or Gites and continued to do so for the rest of the season.

There is plenty of short, medium and long term accommodation to choose from in Chamonix but most of the long term stuff is snapped up by seasonaires who began planning their season in the Alps long before I did.

Oh, there are plenty of share flat options but be prepared to share a one or two bedroom apartment with three to eight or more people. You can easily tell who these people are when you are out drinking as many of them chose not to wait for the shower as making happy hour is far more of the essence than washing their clothes. It is easy to pick the ski bums who have been seasonaires since they can remember - often by their teeth. A dentist with a passion for skiing could make good money in the Alps.

If you are not picky, and prepared to pay top dollar, there are lots of accommodation options at the high end. I looked at a pile of studios and one bedroom apartments that looked like something out of a third world country but they were incredibly expensive. I saw nothing less than 600 Euros per month and for that price it was a studio which reminded me of Nelson Mandela's prison cell and in the worst part of town, Chamonix Sud – an area comparable to any poor or council high rise housing you will find in the slums of any big city but Detroit is what comes to mind. The only thing going for it is a few good bars, restaurants, and excellent panorama views and the fact that for some reason the Swedish seem to love the place and that is where the majority of them live. Perhaps that is why the prices are so ludicrous for what you get but hey this is a world class ski resort.

As I mentioned earlier there are bargains but they have been rented weeks if not months before I got there. I certainly saw another side of Chamonix looking at apartments. It was clearly evident that there was a distinct demand for accommodation and thus ruthless landlords could get away with charging the earth. So I gave up looking for accommodation - it is soul destroying and wastes way too much time. It turned out to be absolutely the right move as I met a tonne of people who otherwise I never would. It also meant I could move closer to whichever chalet I was cooking at which saved a tonne of time driving.

That night I started working at Chalet Le Marti. My initial impression of the chalet business was an optimistic one nonetheless and I was suitably impressed with Le Marti - it had all the bells and whistles you would expect from a luxury chalet, it was more like a boutique hotel. The chalet is co-managed by George from Dynamic lives and Jamie Strachan (owner and manager of a very up-market business called Hip Chalets). He came to Chamonix many years ago as a professional free skier and stayed like many others and now his business is one of the most successful in town catering to the rich and famous.

Le Marti used to be a boutique hotel and restaurant and boasted eight en-suite bedrooms, a sauna, spa, five staff, its own transport and a private chef – Dom with whom I would be working. An Englishman he had worked in the area for the last eight years. He was fantastic to work with and by the end of the week he had not only shown me the ropes such as where to buy the best produce, meats, seafood, vegetables, cheeses, cured meats and daily freshly baked bread but also given me a wonderful introduction and insight into the chalet business in Chamonix.

Dom had cooked for literally thousands of guests during his eight year span and was now breaking into the fashion business with his wife and was continuing to cook to support himself. His snowboard clothing label was already selling quite well. He told me stories of tips large enough to take a long holiday with but he also told me about nightmare clients that were never satisfied with the luxurious surroundings, food or service.

In addition to Dom's information I had heard umpteen stories about the business but like anything, you can beat firsthand experience. There were three chalet hosts, a manager and a driver. The manger Emma and her driver fiancée, Ben had put their successful careers in event management and motorboat racing on hold to have their much anticipated season in the Alps. They were a marvellous couple; attractive, outgoing, with a tremendous sense of humour and always positive no matter how much shit was thrown at them.

I liked them both immediately and although quite a lot younger than me they were easily my favourite couple of the season. We were to have many a late night on the town where we would share stories about guests and laugh at how peculiar many of them were. The three young girls who were the chalet hosts at Le Marti had worked at a similar upmarket chalet in Verbier the previous season and your first impression was that working in a chalet was the last thing in the world they actually wanted to do - and I could see why; it's genuinely hard work.

The most common package is that a chalet girl/host will get paid up to 100 Euros a week; with their accommodation and ski lift pass also taken care of, but this is not always the case. I occasionally worked with a permanent seasonal employee of Dynamic Lives who got paid 90 Euros a week but still had to pay for her accommodation which meant she was in debt at the end of each month and had to make up the difference by praying for tips. That really sucked but she continued working the whole season complaining to everyone apart from George.

I soon found that chalet hosts are often just out of school and this is their first time away from home and it is a matter of opinion as to what is fair and what is not. A chalet owner or manager will generally tell you that chalet hosts are lazy and all they are here for is to ski and socialise whilst the hosts refer to themselves as chalet slaves which, as you can imagine, cannot be the best for anyone's self esteem.

Personally I think anyone is harebrained to take a job as a chalet host unless you are one of the very, very few that find a good balance between work and play and I can tell you those positions are as rare as hens' teeth. But for someone who has never left home before this will soon get you into shape, if not make you very cynical about the world to come. My advice is that you should save up and get some experience working in a restaurant or bar which will allow you ample amounts of time to ski and explore the area especially as there is so much to do and see.

These three young chalet hosts at Le Marti detested their jobs but certainly loved the night-life Argentiere offered and soon developed an almost local celebrity like status for their late night exploits - which have to be commended on 90 Euros a week (you work the rest out). After many warnings the leader of the group was fired so they all packed up their bags and left town never to be seen of or heard of again. They probably just turned up at the next resort and started their antics again.

Back at Le Marti, I was quickly learning how cooking in the chalet business worked and what type of food I would probably end up preparing. It seemed easy enough to me. As the kitchen at Le Marti had been set up initially as a restaurant it was a dream to work in. It had a large gas oven, fryer, char-grill and hot plate. It had all the kitchen utensils you could possibly wish for and more and there was plenty of dry storage and freezer space downstairs in the large basement. Unfortunately it gave me a false sense of security as none of the other seven chalets I was to work in were a match to this standard of luxury.

The chalet business in Chamonix usually worked on a fly into Geneva on a Saturday and out the following Saturday. As chef it was my job to email the client for their food requirements and then confirm their weekly menu over the phone. Menu planning was therefore reasonably easy depending on their food requirements which I found out later could be vegetarian, vegan or Halal. The hours were long: up at 6am pick up the fresh baguettes and croissants at 6.30am, start breakfast prep at 6.45am, cooking at 7.30am, serve breakfast at 8.00am. Tidy up at 9.00am, bake a cake around 10.00am and then start preparation at around 3.00pm for the evening meal – which could be served anywhere from 6.00pm to 9.00pm.

Baking a cake for afternoon tea seemed really stupid to me as I had been skiing all this time and have never eaten cake afterwards! I was told it is an English thing - cake and tea and all that sort of stuff. Well I baked plenty of cakes and some would try them but they were seldom ever finished. Dinner was usually four courses and you would be up as late as the guests were. Many of the chefs I met never seemed to fit in much skiing but I made an effort to get up the mountain every day even if it was just for two to three hours.

Food requirements could often stuff up your day such as the first group at Le Marti only ate Halal. Dom and I had to drive for about an hour and a half to find a Halal butcher which was closed when we got there – a valuable lesson in not forgetting that almost every business in France closes from 12 to 2.30pm for lunch.

Our group were from England but all of Pakistan origin and a terrific bunch. I had a tiptop time with them, and they were an excellent introduction to the chalet business. They were all keen movie goers and I ran a quiz evening for them which was a big hit even though I was later to be told off for getting too close to the customer: give me a break. There were strict policies on how to deal with all clients with which I did not agree at all from day one but any business needs to have rules I guess.

I can only compare it to staying in a good hotel where they call you sir and madam in a robotic sort of way with no feeling or genuineness at all. New Zealanders are well-known for their friendly demeanour and some silly little chalet company was not going to change a national tradition, you would have a better chance of holding back the tide! This however is not the case with the way other chalets are managed. There are many operators where the chef actually sits down and eats with the guests as well as skiing and socialising with them. I am told these chalets get better tips, which makes perfect sense to me.

Dom continued to share his wealth of knowledge with me, which was much appreciated and I would have been in deep shit without his help. He also took me to Metro which is the large French restaurant/hotel wholesaler/cash and carry which sells absolutely everything from fresh produce, dairy, local and international meats, fresh seafood, fruit and vegetables, bulk foods and the very latest catering equipment. I could also buy New Zealand lamb, Australian and Argentinean grain fed beef and live lobster from one of their many tanks.

The wines and spirits area was as good as I had ever seen and I have since become friends with the sommelier who has taken great pleasure in educating me about French wines. Our first visit was a little rushed but on my next visit I almost spent an entire day familiarizing myself with the football field size wholesaler. There are 19 Metros throughout France which service the very best and some of the most famous restaurants to be found anywhere on the globe. To become a member (it's a very much the French way of doing things) there is a stringent administration and acceptance process.

The guests at Le Marti that week wanted home cooked food as many of the clients do. I found that many people that come to the Alps have lifestyles that pertain to eating out at restaurants on a regular basis and when at home they have joined the revolution of pre-packed cooked meals as they are quick, easy and require no effort or thought. When they come to the Alps they want to get back to their origins and eat what mum cooked at home. We are a simple species really!

I spent the week at Le Marti and on Dom's day off had the guests to myself, which was a little nerve racking, but I got through the day without any major problems cooking four courses for twelve adults as well as their children. I was already having a blast and enjoying the local nightlife of the area and familiarising myself with Argentiere's half dozen or so bars as well as the local food.

It often snowed and the setting could not have been more picturesque. One of the local elders had died during my tenure at Le Marti and one morning about 100 conservatively darkly-dressed locals walked through deep snow in unison to the graveyard which was very close to the chalet, behind the historic church. It was a postcard setting, so much so that you could easily get away with selling tickets – I doubt many people would have seen a funeral like it at all. It was snowing heavily and it looked like a scene out of a Sergio Leone movie.

> *"The first fall of snow is not only an event, it is a magical event. You go to bed in one kind of a world and wake up in another quite different, and if this is not enchantment then where is it to be found?"*
> **J.B. Priestley**

What I was to especially relish during the season was the consistent precipitation of snow. I have always loved snow since it first snowed in Twizel when I moved there as a child: first snow man; monolithic snow fights at school where you would be sent home due to being soaked through; first sled ride and of course the first time skiing. I hold dear that first time of the year when you put your tongue out and catch a large flake as it melts signifying the start of winter. I still love skiing just as much when it is snowing, taking long walks or having a meal or drink with friends to the backdrop of snowflakes glittering, glistening and gleaming.

I did not come to Chamonix to find romance but do weather patterns provide anything more romantic than an angel crying; ha. Seriously snow is magical as it absorbs the sound and brings out the child in the most jaded of souls; it's mysterious, ethereal, joyful and timeless – it's the purest gem of surpassing beauty as snowflakes gently float from heaven to earth. It's clean, pure and refreshing. Sue, who you will meet later in the book, and I loved to sit for hours at the window table of Le Dahu Hotel having a long boozy lunch and just watch the snow fall as we tried to find the best way to describe the flakes falling.

Certainly we agreed the whole world changes, it moves into another dimension and we both loved the delicious crunch of fresh snow under foot. The regular snow fall was the perfect medicine for me – I find it cleansing, giving me a sense of renewal. Even the Chamonix South grotto looked beautiful when it snowed. I also loved walking home after a few drinks with the snow falling heavily as I gathered my thoughts and smiled lucking myself for being in the Alps.

There is a book titled Snow Crystals by W.A. Bentley (1865 - 1931) who took over 5000 photos of different snow crystals through a photographic microscope. 2,453 are shown in his book - an incredible feat as they are almost impossible to capture on film and their photography is a very difficult and tricky procedure. It has to be, as it can only be achieved in the extreme cold. The lighting must be perfect without producing a hint of heat that will melt the snowflake. He was the first person to introduce the world to the beauty, complexity and diversity of snow crystals and many have followed in his footsteps.

It snowed consistently throughout January and February throughout the valley and there was always snow on the road. You would often have to dig your car out of and I never did get around to buying snow tyres for Charlie or snow chains for that matter. I had a couple of close calls but even in the deepest snow he would get through it but I put that down to buying Charlie off a farmer who put good farm tyres on him.

Other folk were not so lucky and almost every day you would see accidents caused by drivers who didn't have the foggiest clue how to drive in control in snow hazard conditions.

The Chamonix Police would often have road blocks out checking for snow chains and snow tyres but I never got checked and they always let me through. Driving at night when it is snowing heavily was always a fun experience as you feel like you are driving in space. It was a blissful way to spend time and also to test Charlie's capabilities.

> *"When it is moderately cold and rainy, snow falls as little rose thorns and tiny grains. When the cold moderates, snow falls like stars with many points like ferns... In severe cold, without wind snow falls like stars with clusters, because they are not separated by wind."*
> **Frederich Martens 1671**

During my week at Le-Marti I stayed at Le Dahu Hotel which is the second oldest hotel in Argentiere and traditionally French. Antique alpine gear was hung on the walls with old art and photos depicting the rich history of the village. People used to farm ice here and carry it back as far as Paris and London on horse drawn carriages to be used in restaurants, hotels and for fish markets.

The cuisine at Le Dahu Hotel was excellent and very local as well as very reasonably priced. The bubbly staff, which consisted of mainly mature, outgoing, women were fantastic. Very few of them spoke English and even if they did they preferred to speak French. They were a ton of fun.

The restaurant seated about 120 and was always full for lunch and dinner and it is mostly occupied by French customers. I treasured it, especially the atmosphere and lively French spirit of the place. I am glad I stayed there as it is easy to forget you are in France when you are in Chamonix as it is so international and full of English speaking people. I have been back many times over the season and have not been disappointed in the cuisine or the service. For 15 Euros you could get a three course lunch or dinner which was the best value for money I was to find all season. Sue and I would often order six different dishes and it was a feast that was hard to finish – oh and they serve the wine in clay jugs that are very bona fide.

After a week working with Dom I was set to have first customers of my own and it was to be like that from now on. My first clients were a young and very successful IT businessman, his stunning Swedish wife and sister-in-law from Monaco. They had a one year old baby so they could not venture out to restaurants easily and so had chosen a private chef – me!

They had rented a very up market three bedroom apartment just below the Brevant lift. Although perfectly located there was hardly enough room to throw a cat and the dining table was about a meter from the open plan kitchen. But they wanted no expense spared so I suggested a variety of dishes which I thought they would never go for, such as black truffles with fresh scampi, Gordon Ramsay's pan seared Foie Gras with a citrus glaze, lobster risotto, aged fillet of Australian grain fed beef with a red wine and thyme reduction and New Zealand spring lamb leg stuffed with goats cheese and fresh mint.

I thought if I could pull this off in a tiny kitchen then cooking anything else during the season would be a breeze. Well, rest assured they went for everything and I had a ball cooking several dishes I had only ever eaten in expensive French restaurants. It was a wondrous week especially as it snowed most nights.

It also prompted my first confrontation with George - which was to be one of many. I had seen the way he shouted at and abused his chalet hosts and now he was yelling at me as the kitchen wasn't tidy when he visited. But, as I tried to point out, it was because there was no hot water and the sink was always blocked. I felt sorry for the clients. It was Christmas week and they had paid a small fortune to rent the apartment which had a problem sink and despite the fact there were only three adults, every day one of them could not shower as there was no hot water left. It really was outrageous but George's come back was it was the landlords fault as he only rented the apartment from a local French family. He had a valid point and it was hard to work out where the responsibility lay but it certainly wasn't with the clients. That aside I had a tremendous time with the guests especially as I was in their face at all times.

Everyone who is new in the chalet business like me is given a damned rushed introduction mainly due to timing and demand. The first surge is Christmas week and then its New Years week and there is hardly time to breath in-between. They say if you can survive these two crucial weeks you should be fine for the rest of the season but by the end of the two weeks there is high staff turnover for sure.

On Christmas day I spent the day skiing. As I had been consumed in cooking and quickly trying to adapt my style to luxury chalet chef for the first week and a half I had still not made it to the slopes.

Being a real Christmas person, and loving all things Christmas-like, I had always dreamed of skiing Christmas day and there is definitely something magical about it especially as it snowed most of the day. The conditions were shocking but I was in heaven being in the snow no matter what. I also enjoyed a superb lunch at Le Bergerie at the top of the Planpraz bubble lift at Brevant. It was a sublime way to spend the day and I thought a lot about my unsurpassed friends and life back in New Zealand where I had spent many Christmases at their seaside beach houses enjoying a few ice cold beers while cooking up a storm over an open home-made BBQ with a menu of eating paua (abalone), crayfish or a few good lamb chops or sausages.

I was glad however to finally put my old life behind me as I sat there cogitating my new one the Chamonix alpine experience was offering me. I thought if I hadn't come to Chamonix my life would have continued as it had, full of attractive people and congenial events, it would have been so pleasant a life I never could have comprehended my own sadness. Chamonix gave me the perfect opportunity and anonymity to contemplate and to turn my life around. Do you ever find you get caught up in some sort of social, work or relationship trap and it's almost impossible to get off the treadmill? I did.

Even though I have lived a pretty full life to date and have terrific lifelong friends, I hated myself before I came to Chamonix. I hated who I had become and I had previously fallen into the deepest bout of depression that I did not know was possible and was completely unhappy.

I was doing everything for the wrong reasons and my unhappiness was the result. But, as I have already mentioned, I had found a new love and that is writing but, more importantly, writing about what I love. I was listening to one of Anthony Robins personal development tapes some years ago in his "Get the Edge" series and something I have never forgot was that when he was in his deepest despair, broke, alone and suicidal he was told by a respected elder that he had nothing to worry about as his gifts would set him free and everything you have done to date will determine your future.

So considering my similar predicament I started writing and I have not stopped for a couple of years. There is never a day that goes by now where I am not writing, taking notes or creatively thinking. I started with two screenplays, my book on movies and a novel I am writing at the same time at this. Writing this book has transformed me from being very depressed to a level of happiness and contentment I did not know was possible.

"I've come to believe that all my past failure and frustrations were actually laying the foundation for the understandings that have created the new level of living I now enjoy."
Tony Robins

Had I not come to Chamonix and spent such a length of time in the Alps I would not have been able to give myself such a positive mental, emotional and physical transformation. I did not need the Prozac the doctor had put me on. I did not need any medication or counselling; I just needed to get away from the shallow and unhappy existence I was living. For me it was now all about resetting life boundaries and doing what it is that makes me absolutely happy. Enter the world of snow skiing.

I don't know how to pinpoint it, but the Alps are the perfect place to reflect. Words once again can't describe how good it felt to be up there by myself on Christmas day and in such solitude. I was so happy to be out of the city where only a handful of people really understood me or for that matter really cared about me. But I also came to Chamonix because I was searching strenuously for new people, adventure and experience.

I sat there that Christmas Day reflecting over the last 25 years in business including 17 years in hospitality with nothing to show for it in the financial sense. Indeed it was dispiriting but not lonely. Honestly I thought I never loved the restaurant business which I had recently failed in financially. Not deeply, not for long. I found them wearisome after they were all set up and running. Sure I was passionate about them at times but I never once thought they were my calling in life. As romantic and idealistic as owning a restaurant sounds they are one hell of a tough business to own and manage.

I have some good friends who are the some of the most successful restaurant operators in New Zealand and their commitment and passion is something I admired but never could find in myself. I have had the same problems in business as with relationships, the initial infatuation, the honeymoon period, having to work at it, then boredom and losing interest, then the break-up. I also knew my failings were my own choice motivated by an inner dissatisfaction, a lack of creativity and a deficiency of personal development which I could only find in skiing, movies and writing which is as far from being in the limelight or socialising as you can get.

I had built up something of a tall poppy profile and image in New Zealand through 16 years as a film reviewer on radio and was the New Zealand's sole accredited press representative at seven Cannes film festivals amongst many others. I hosted my own regional television show for a couple of years and was a wine writer and freelance writer for a series of high profile magazines and newspapers as well as being the host, MC or organiser of high profile events and occasions. I even stood for Mayor of Wellington and launched a very successful and high profile campaign until the local media and a jealous brother starting attacking me and diminished any hope. I was a well-known socialite and as one five star restaurant review I received described me as the Andy Warhol of Wellington who was seen at every event even at the opening of an envelope. I don't think my lifestyle could have possibly been more shallow and empty.

I had lost every cent I had in the world, the girl I supposedly loved no longer loved me and as a result I was made a laughing stock in the New Zealand media and amongst many of the shallow fickle people I once called friends.

> *"Be more concerned with your character than your reputation, because your character is what you really are, while your reputation is merely what others think you are."*
> **John Wooden**

"Hallelujah!" How lucky was I for all this to happen and as I looked back I had an overwhelmingly sense of complete freedom and gratitude for a second chance to finally follow my dreams.

> *"Only when you lose everything, are you free to do anything."*
> **Chuck Palahniuk, Fight Club**

What it took to get me to this stage I wish on no man but here I was away from the life I hated, living a life I had only ever imagined. The more I thought about it the more I realised that my only problems were financial and that is nothing more than a temporary inconvenience.

I felt glad that I had the opportunity to turn my life around once and for all. I stopped worrying about all the negative press I was getting back home and turned all my attention to the future. All I had to do was take a look around to know fate had brought me to the perfect place to find the strength and fulfilment I was looking for. I wanted to be fascinated with life again, I wanted to discover, to be curious and renew my lust for life by renewing my spirit the only way I knew how; through adventure.

It started to snow heavily as I scribbled down the notes I am re-writing now and I got back on my skis and skied into the abyss. You know sometimes you have to remind yourself that it's okay to feel good and skiing is the perfect reminder as being on the mountain outweighs any misery.

> *"Like success, failure is many things to many people. With a positive mental attitude failure is a learning experience, a rung on the ladder, a plateau at which you get your thoughts in order and prepare to try again."*
> **W. Clement Stone**

With a couple of glasses of cheap French Burgundy in the system I hit the steeper slopes and let it rip like there was no tomorrow through the snow clad pine trees. There were only a few people on the mountain as skiing fast is very dangerous if it is crowded. I wanted to really get the adrenalin pumping to release as many endorphins into my system as possible while I was trying to control my fear. I can tell you there is plenty of fear skiing with gear you have never used before on a slope you have never skied. But I was up for it and the more I pushed myself against my own barriers the bigger the buzz I felt. The more you push yourself skiing you know that there is an increased level of risk and it's very addictive. I fell many times and laughed out loud as I continued looking like the Abominable Snowman.

Controlling your fear is a capacious mind game and it's what skiing is all about for me as it's where the real joy comes from. I had not skied this year in New Zealand as I had worked around the clock to finish my movie book - so being back on skis was a real blast and I caught the very last lift at 4.30pm. Feeling elated and very much in the Christmas spirit of things I enjoyed every second of the last run with a couple of pisters (Chamonix Ski Patrol) closing the mountain behind me. They looked at me as if I was a little mad but we all had a good laugh to the top wishing each other Merry Christmas in French, German and English.

After skiing I went into Chamonix to the Mix Bar with George and Ed for a glass of champagne. Ed reminded me of Fuzzy Bear from the Muppets due to his bushy red curly hair and winning smile which never seemed to leave his face. He was to be the most social of anyone I met throughout the up and coming season. He was about 25 and had taken time out from the start of his successful career working as a banker for

Macquarie Bank in Australia to have a season in the French Alps as a driver for Dynamic Lives. This was one of the few nights he kept his shirt on!

We ventured through a peppy street atmosphere to a restaurant of that exact name which George had obviously had a very good relationship with as the owner treated us to plenty of fabulous Rose Champagne. On the way back home I once again slipped on bloody ice and put my hand out to stop the fall and ended up with a nasty cut that probably should have been stitched. No matter how much salt or grit they put everywhere the new ice would still be slippery!

Later that evening I made it back to the hostel I had booked into the day before - the tourist office told me it was the only accommodation available in the whole of Chamonix. The tourist office website is linked into all the accommodation on offer and on any given day they can tell you what is available and where, which is pretty damn good considering there are 67,000 individual beds available on any given night.

Back at the hostel, which slept 100 and looked like a large Swiss chalet, I ended up cooking left over black truffles with local Tom Savoie melted cheese and baguette for a bunch of people I had met from all over the planet. The guests from Monaco I was cooking for had bought me a sublime bottle of Bordeaux and the cheese which really added to my Christmas cheer (it was the only present I had been given as not even my mother knew exactly where I was at that stage). We sat around a large long table and shared our food, wine and stories of our alpine adventures. I had been in Chamonix less than two weeks and had already met people from at least 15 different countries.

It was only later that we found out that a 43 year old British skier had died that day at La Tour. La Tour is the easiest of the ski areas you can ski in Chamonix and it was a shock to find out that on my first day on the slopes someone had died. I found out also that the 43 year old was a keen skier who was skiing with his girlfriend and other friends he was sharing the festive season with. He had decided to do one last run and was found the next day just five meters off piste in a snow drift which was also reported as a small avalanche.

The conditions on Christmas day were horrendous with high winds, no visibility as well as continuous snow drifts. He was found with no avalanche transceiver on him which probably would have saved his life. God, to think I was skiing in the same conditions by myself without an avalanche transceiver - it just as easily could have been me. Anyone skiing by themselves in those conditions is without a doubt taking their life into their own hands no matter how experienced they are. You can only imagine what sort of Christmas his girlfriend and friends had after that. There was a heated debate over the death which was the second at La Tour that week.

There was no doubt that people were becoming more wary of La Tour as its safety record is appalling. It is perceived as an easy ski area which has readily accessible off piste terrain, something which coerces the inexperienced skier into attempting them unprepared and often in unsuitable conditions. The response from mountain safety is that while they are sorry such incidents occur it is a simple fact that some skiers are absolutely ignorant of basic safety rules and unfortunately statistics show that most avalanche deaths happen close to the piste.

Unfortunately such occurrences were to become a part of everyday life living in the high Alps. I was told and found it very hard to believe but throughout the year there is an average of one death per day in the Chamonix Mont Blanc region. That includes all deaths through activities such as skiing, climbing, hiking and even walking at altitude.

The next week was New Year's Eve and George had booked me with one of his best clients and seven of his friends at Chalet Le Mouilles. It was another stunning chalet where I stayed a few nights before finding accommodation. It was a very old farm house that was only recently converted into a chalet. From the spa there were perfect views of Mont Blanc. It had all the mod cons including a state of the art electric induction oven operated by a magnet. The group were a bunch of professional and very well educated gay men in their late 30s and early forties with an overwhelmingly experienced wine palate.

The ritual for the week was the very best champagne (often vintage) after skiing while the leader of the bunch would play Mozart concertos on the piano that he had brought with him. His mother was an opera singer and from the age of five this little maestro would play for mother in concerts. He was ridiculously talented which extended to his extreme skiing and high ranking position in merchant banking in London and New York. They would then sauna and spa before breaking out the serious wines which I would endeavour to match with the food I cooked. I put on my black dinner suit for New Year's Eve and served up a storm. It felt great putting on a suit in the Alps. Cooking breakfast and dinner for guests for seven days becomes quite personal and you do get a complete impression of how the other half lives.

During the day (31ˢᵗ Dec) I had caught up with a fellow New Zealander and Wellingtonian, Matt Whittaker who was ending an OE with a season in Chamonix and then heading home to start taking life a bit more seriously by working and eventually running the family business - New Zealand's most successful chocolate company Whittaker's.

Matt is one of those guys that people seemed to flock around. Tallish, dark and handsome with a positive demeanour he made new friends easily with his affable outgoing personality and baritone voice. He was currently dating a beautiful Dior model he'd met at one of Chamonix's chintzy bars. We met at the Bar Des Sports in the middle of Chamonix where I had sat down after almost breaking my back a few weeks earlier.

The bistro/bar has been popular with mountain guides and ski instructors for years and if you wanted to find a guide in days gone by you would go to places like Bar Des Sports, network, talk to the staff and before you knew it you would be half way up Mont Blanc.

Matt had a wide range of options in choosing where to spend the ski season. He and some friends from New Zealand he was flatting with in Chamonix had previously had a full season in Canada. Like many experienced snowboarders he was attracted to the off piste action Chamonix had to offer as well as the scintillating social scene. I joined Matt and his bonny sister Holly, who was visiting from London, later that evening in Chamonix square to welcome in the New Year. Holly reminded me of a young Elizabeth Taylor when she starred in Father of the Bride with Spencer Tracey. I was fully taken by her but unfortunately such a melody was not to be written on this occasion. Never mind, her company was just what the doctor ordered!

There were thousands of people in the square to welcome in the New Year and the atmosphere was comparable to the likes of Times Square, fires works and the like but with the background of Mont Blanc. I felt a touch of loneliness being away from my close bunch of friends back home but Matt, Holly and a bunch of their friends were marvellous company. We ventured to one of Chamonix's most famous bars Chambre Neuf. It is Swedish owned and run and was filled to the brim including plenty of stunning Scandinavians dancing on every table - it was almost like being in a bar in Stockholm. The atmosphere was electric and I met plenty of people who were there for the entire season that I would later bump into on a semi-regular basis.

Being in Chamonix alone for the winter season I was not sure how much I would enjoy Christmas and New Year's Eve but surprisingly I felt quite at home - everybody it seemed was in the same boat as me seeking a higher adventure than their previous life had offered them. It only seemed like yesterday when I would have a beautiful bod beside me in a similar packed bar in some ski resort in New Zealand where I would be the life and soul of the party – here I was just another face in the crowd and treated accordingly and I loved every second of it.

Consciously or unconsciously you come to the mountains for the full winter season as you have been contemplating life in some way or another or like many you are just another adrenalin junkie who needs a daily fix - addicts are addicts no matter what the physiological condition or dependence. In the mountains you are addicted to the rush, facing your fears and then overcoming them by pushing yourself to your limits and beyond. But those limits change the more you push them, confidence grows and when you get to that stage like many of the people that are attracted to Chamonix you are playing with more than fire. Welcome to the world of hard core I thought as my mind worked overtime trying to find some sensibility in coming to Chamonix.

In Chamonix there is little talk of what you do outside skiing, certainly never talk of where you went to school and rarely who your friends are or who you know – it's a great leveller. It would be a perfect place for a criminal to hide as no one really gives a damn about who you are. Everyone just wants to talk skiing or boarding and to relive their adventures or to find out what's hot and what's not on the slopes. It's like; let's put life on hold for a while because whatever is going on in the world is not that important.

That night I was invited to a party at one of the associated companies superfine chalets called The Farm House where they had Kylie Minogue staying. She had flown in a bunch of her jet set friends and it was "the party" and not to be missed but I was having a ball where I was and didn't come to Chamonix to star gaze. I was finding a common denominator with everyone I was talking with and I was sure Kylie and I had little to catch up over.

What became obvious to me about the people I was meeting in Chamonix is that all of them were looking for challenges as they wanted to overcome something in themselves, and like me they wanted to find something that is bigger than them but still part of them. Every second person I talked with shared similar thoughts and stories of why they were there for the season. I soon found out that in the Chamonix area more than anywhere else in the world people play with death every day, they play with the meaning of life and they play with their destiny. They play with who they are and their connection to nature which I found fascinating.

Don't you agree that life and society is doing everything possible to take us away from nature? I was spell-bound by many of these tales and it fuelled my determination to write this book - the consummate way to make the very most of the winter season and give me an excuse to meet even more of the people that have made Chamonix the legendary place it is. And, if nobody else reads it apart from my mother, then I will have fully indulged in my new passion and maybe even improved my writing.

It turns out to be an astonishingly cracking New Year's Eve and once again I feel a strong sense on contentment in making the decision to spend a season here. Foolishly I drove Holly back to Matt's apartment. The roads were like driving on an ice skating rink as they had frozen over and it had started to snow heavily as well. There were cars crag-fast on each side of the road when one suddenly pulled out in front of me. Naturally, but foolishly, I hit the brakes and Charlie somehow glides past four cars in a 360 degree spin and misses them all. The music of Johann Strauss would have been the perfect symphony for such an occasion. Matt and I look at each other with relief and burst out laughing. That was the last time I risked such an escapade. If I had hit one of the cars I would have been in deep shit and would have ended up spending the night in a cold concrete cell not to mention the fine and damages I would have had to pay. Such decisions can ruin a season and see you on the next plane home - unfortunately such incidents happen often.

Our last port of call is to join a bunch of Matt's friends at Le Vagabond which is a legendary 150 year old stone hotel that is now a voguish hostel. Over 100 years ago coaches used to stop there on route to Switzerland. Now it is one of the hippest hostels in France with regular international DJs and as their website depicts the place is lively, upbeat and friendly. It reminded me of a bar in Sydney I used to frequent when I lived there called Lo-tel. Le Vagabond proves to as eventful a venue as you would hope to anywhere on the planet that night. It was the ultimate way to finish my New Year's Eve bender. It was almost dawn as I left Charlie and staggered back in the chilling cold a couple of miles to the chalet to cook breakfast for seven very hung-over but surprisingly cheerful gay men. One did however notice that I was still wearing my dinner suit as I served him his truffle omelette!

I gave my first ski lesson on New Year's Day to one of my clients and as he was very fit and lacked fear, he progressed very quickly which was encouraging for me. I was not actually meant to be giving lessons as you have to be employed by one of the local ski schools. If I was caught my season pass could be confiscated and I could also have been fined. At the other extreme if you are caught either ski or mountain guiding in Chamonix without the legal requirements or qualifications you can be thrown in jail for some time and banned for life. I was told of many examples of this happening as ski guiding is quite lucrative.

Chamonix is a very small place and rumours spread faster than an avalanche that a particular rock star and her friends had a complete bender for a few days, eating little while aiding the local underworld out of the recession. Tiger Woods' wife was also staying in one of the top chalets in the valley but alas she was nowhere to be found out socialising or even on the slopes. So, she was not there to find a new husband - damn it!

The recession has had a major impact on both the chalet and ski business as skiing is once again classified as a luxury pastime. Every bar, restaurant and hotel only a few years ago were all full to the brim. But skiing is an expensive sport. The recession also had a major impact on the corporate event business with many companies going bankrupt.

Statistics show that most people that come to Chamonix, by far come for just a week. The majority of these people that come for a week either stay in some type of hotel, chalet, apartment, guest house or hostel. Most people that come hire their ski gear but they still have to buy the rest of their ski clothing that they will seldom use. There are quite a few people that only ever ski or board a week a year and they own all their own gear. My one and only point is that skiing on average is the most expensive sport in relation to spend by comparison to the time spent actually doing it so my conclusions is, do more of it to justify such expenditure.

"The sport of skiing consists of wearing three thousand dollars worth of clothes and equipment and driving two hundred miles in the snow in order to stand around a bar and get drunk."
P.J. O'Rourke

Over the entire season I worked in seven different luxury chalets and gave ski lessons to many of my clients. The majority of my guests were from the UK but I also cooked for people from Monaco, Sweden, Norway, Ireland, Belgium, Japan, South Korea, Scotland, Wales, Russia, the US, Canada, Australia and even George's brother and family from New Zealand.

Dynamic Lives had a strict policy of little or no personal contact with clients and to keep everything what they called "totally professional". Staff were threatened with being dismissed if they were caught drinking with a client or seen socialising with them in one of the local bars. It was like working for a five star Swiss hotel and after 17 years working in hospitality I disagreed with George completely - whose banking background meant he had never owned a bar or restaurant. I got to know all my clients well. I cooked for them, skied with them, socialised with them and occasionally got a little drunk with them but more importantly established friendships with them. I had a grand time getting to know people from all walks of life with many (apart from the seven gay men) inviting me to visit if I was ever in their neck of the woods.

I also made exceptional tips and all these things combined drove George prodigiously mad. Had I not been a freelancer the chalet staff told me I would have been long gone but chefs were in demand and by the end of the season he only gave me work if he had no other choice.

George had hired me as a freelance chef because of the impact of the recession and previously most large chalets would have a permanent chef assigned to it. I looked at such positions and they looked pretty awful, the money was shockingly bad, you had to share a room and most importantly there looked like there was little time for skiing. It never ceases to amaze me how many people are lured to the Alps on such a false sense of security.

George was trying a new concept which meant he would eliminate most of the risk by only providing a chef as an additional service as and when wanted. This made a lot of sense and I could not work out why the concept had not been used more often. Over the season I was to meet many chefs who had once been permanent but due to economics were now employed on a free lance basis. It was certainly a sign of the times.

I liked George but I took little notice of him as the more I saw of the way he ran his business the greater amount of regard I lost for him. There were always problems with the chalets that he would always blame the customer for. There were continuous electrical, plumbing, hot water and fire starting problems and he treated his chalet hosts like cheap whores. In George's defence he was only financially involved in one of the chalets but he still managed the others and thus the responsibility lay with him.

I saw staff come and go on a regular basis a result of the huge gap of expectation between employers and the chalet staff and this was consistent with everyone I talked to. The first chalet manager George hired–a young New Zealand girl with a degree in marketing had never worked in the business before–she was so battered and bruised by his constant abuse the poor thing quit and tried chalet hosting for a while until she eventually got a real job back in London. Her leaving party was the best of season and during her last few days you could see the sparkle and vitality that had been quashed by the tediousness of her job returning. And funnily enough, George was nowhere to be seen.

We were meant to be offering a luxury chalet experience but none of the chalet hosts had any hospitality experience - to the extent some did not even know how to set up a table for dinner. I thought this was ridiculous but is was certainly indicative of the chalet business and staff were prepared to work for next to nothing and thus unqualified people were hired.

The first chalet manager was replaced by a war horse career chalet manager with plenty of experience. This close to 40 year old English woman left school and worked in the chalet business and never left apart from working on boats in the Mediterranean in summer. Her business card stated that she was the resort manager. One had to wonder what resort she was talking about, certainly not Club Med.

The weathering and scars of this choice of career were evident to everyone apart from her. I felt sorry for the other chalet staff as they had to share the same quarters. The day she arrived at the staff accommodation she totally rearranged the furniture, cleaned and then gave the staff a lecture on the new standards of cleanliness and hygiene she expected. When she did drink her personality would take on something comparable to a Werewolf and look out if you got in the way with spurts of violence and loud screams of abuse.

It got to the stage that when she was chatting up a young snowboarder half her age he had a confrontation with her and after that we never really saw her out again and he was kept in free drinks for some time to come. There was no doubt that she has deep down physiological issues and after a few runs in with her over the cleanliness of a blasted oven which she expected me to clean with a toothbrush, I managed to have as little as possible to do with her.

For her finding a few crumbs on the oven wall was like she had just solved the worlds' worst crime and she was full of glee. The reason I mention her is that there are many like her who came for a season and never really left. I can't understand what she likes about the work apart from the power play of being in charge of a few chalet hosts and the guests.

It was very seldom that she ever got to ski but she certainly loved her job and excelled in it.

The BBC made a successful reality television series about chalet hosting as the general public were interested in seeing just how badly treated chalet hosts are and what goes on behind the scenes in world famous ski resorts. It certainly shows the bleak side of human nature but that is what keeps television stations in business I guess. The comparison to the majestic Alps, the perfect alpine holiday and what really happens in the chalet business is such a stark contrast.

Throughout the season I was to meet umpteen people who had come to Chamonix, worked in the chalet business and never left. Some started at the bottom as a host or driver and were still there. Others managed a chalet or like George had grown their chalet businesses by putting more properties on their books. Some had moved into hospitality like Dave who owned the very popular Office Bar in Argentiere and who arrived and worked as a chalet driver ten years ago.

What I did find is that many people that came to Chamonix to live the dream to ski and work just end up working and skiing very little. When the sun shines for many it is time to make hay and these people ski as much as they did when they came on their annual one week ski holiday. After the ski season they would then have plenty of time to look at the mountains with regret of an unfilled ski season. But at least they are looking at the Alps and not some murky polluted sky, brick lane or the like.

A lot of the chalet companies do not actually own the chalets they simply manage a business by renting the chalet from a landlord. Many locals move and rent out their homes and opt for much cheaper accommodation for the season. The chalet businesses make a variety of deals usually guaranteeing the landlord a certain number of weeks rent throughout the season and then making a profit on the difference and on all of the many extras that are included. Many of the companies are not French but rather English and clients pay in either pounds or Euros. Any fool could do it really even if you don't speak a word of French as it's not exactly rocket science. But, to do it well, takes years of experience and hard work especially at the top end of the market.

I had heard many rumours of nightmare clients that came to stay in the chalets with unusual dietary requirements, clients that did not want to see any of the staff, who wanted their linen changed every time they breathed on it and who treated the chalet staff like peasants, demanding to have their milk poured onto their cereal in front of them and such like.

Luckily it was not the case for me, I had some wonderful families and corporate groups who worked in real estate, shipping, finance, banking and IT.

It was fascinating almost living 24/7 with people from such different paths of life who normally I never would have met. If I had not got to know them on a personal basis it would have been an opportunity lost. I also firmly believe, and it is clearly evident, that the Alps bring out the best in people as they come to rehabilitate, reinvigorate, revitalise and rejuvenate. Winter holidays are a source of well being that stays with you all year long. Hasn't the world got it completely wrong that you only get three to four weeks holiday a year?

I enjoyed watching the transition in people over the week; the excitement over dinner as tails were told of their daily adventures. There was often sadness at having to leave at the end of the week especially if there was fresh powder or the sun was out.

> *"Snow: a form of precipitation that usually occurs three weeks prior to and the morning of your departure from your ski vacation."*
> **Anon**

Well often that would be true but there was no shortage of precipitation in Chamonix!

There were of course accidents to contend with. One client, an English woman who did not really want to ski, but had three young sons who were as keen as mustard so she bought them to the slopes every year. I skied with her eldest son who was about 12 and he was a brilliant young skier and I am sure than one day he will ski instruct for a few years before he starts his final studies. This year though her husband did not come as he was a very busy merchant banker and they had recently had a family holiday. Sadly after only few hours on skis she fell and broke her arm so badly she had to be taken to a hospital in Cluses for surgery. Her husband hopped on the next plane and I drove him out to the hospital the next day to see her. He put his busy trading week on hold and took care of the family. We would drink superb Burgundy, eat local meats and cheese during the day getting to know each other while his wife rested and the boys skied. The couple who were close to my age had been together 18 years and every day it was like they were on a first date; I was not sure if the alpine setting had anything to do with it or the accident but my slightly burnt and cynical nature was instilled with hope that there are actually marriages that do work and last in love.

There were plenty of other accidents amongst my clients during the season that I would witness first-hand but nothing too serious. There were broken arms, legs, ribs and plenty of battering and bruises. Clients would come back to the chalets in total shock like they had just had a brief encounter with death. You could see it in their eyes and it was quite scary to say the least. The more accidents I saw the more respect I gained for the mountains as anyone with a little sense would. Often these accidents could have been prevented if the victims had gone to a gym and done some exercise before their week on the slopes but often it also just came down to plain bad luck. It always astonishes me what risks every day people take on the slopes with little expertise or knowledge of the surroundings. The best skiers in the world will tell you again and again to be humble in the mountains, measure your risks and respect the environment.

My advice to anyone renting a chalet would be to do a little research before you commit. It's a buyers' market and there is still an overflow effect from the recession which puts you in the bargaining seat. Deal with a reputable agent or deal with a business that has stood the test of time. If you are after real luxury there are few companies that offer a true five star experience in Chamonix. Hip Chalets is one such company where their guests have included the rich and famous. If you want true luxury with all the trimming go to St Moritz, St Anton, Gstaad, Verbier or Val d'Isere but you will not get the extreme skiing that you will get in Chamonix.

Like Dynamic Lives there are plenty that say they offer luxury but your experience will be reflected in how much you are prepared to spend. As far as hiring a private chef; again it all depends on what you want from your holiday and what you can afford. Unfortunately you don't always get what you pay for and some chalets are shockingly bad with food to match. It also depends what sort of Alpine experience you are seeking but what I can tell you from living here a season is that there are more options in Chamonix than probably anywhere else in the world and that means there are lots of good and a lot of not so good options.

If you want to work in the chalet business all you need is a little hospitality experience and you will easily get a job. It's also worth looking out for pre-season cookery and hostess training courses. As I have pointed out working in a chalet is hard work and it will deprive you of the potential enjoyment and happiness available to you by living and working in the

Alps. Don't be lulled into a false sense of security - you will hardly ever get to see the slopes as much of the work is done when the ski-field is open. I was lucky as I worked as a freelance chef and there was always time to ski even when I was contracted. There is a very acceptable reason why the chalet business has the greatest staff turnover found anywhere on the planet! But hey if it introduces you to the Alps or gets you up there when nothing else will, go for it and enjoy.

Chapter Five
Skiing: HUH! What is it good for?
Absolutely everything!

"*Skiing is a dance and the mountain always leads.*"
Anon

Sports are more than pastimes. They give us the means to reformat our existence, if only briefly into intensely focused events. Sports provide a window to our athletic and adventurous selves. In some sports, the goal is to compete and destroy an opponent's strategy. Some sports focus on teamwork, with each player performing a specific role. But in others, the goal is individual performance, and the players focus internally, charting their progress not by wins or group performance but by their own set of mental expectations. This is the world of the recreational skier. There is a reason why millions of people strap on boards to their feet and slide down snow-covered hills. Skiing is a method of self-discovery. Skiers test themselves and in the process they find both challenges and tranquillity. The sport has it s own kind of magic. But the magic that skiers search for isn't found at the end of the run or at the end of the day but in the midst of things. It's during the process of skiing farther or faster or smoother. With enough time skiing and its movements and rhythms become a kind of dance, a form of expression. Just as an artist paints with an unlimited choice of colours, a complete skier works towards the goal of performance using a wide foundation of skills. Like the artists work, the skiers' quest for personal breakthrough can be ongoing. Many skiers are thirsty for new information and experiences, and the world of skiing is made rich by athletes who don't mind if their search for excellence borders on being a fanatical quest.

The extract above was from the book The All-Mountain Skier by Mark Elling. This book helped my skiing tremendously throughout my season both improving my skiing technique but also in teaching less experienced skiers. The book is aimed at the intermediate to expert skier and I found it much easier to read and understand than the ski instructor manuals and the like. If you do not like reading there is a first-rate set of training DVDs by renowned ski coach Warren Smith that suits all levels that I bought and highly recommend.

I have personally been just crazy about skiing since I first slid those planks down a mountain side in 1976. I had never thought much about skiing until six months earlier when I was living with an aunt and uncle in Wellington New Zealand - even though mum and dad met on a ski trip. My aunt was Dutch but had lived in Switzerland where she had skied for many years. She filled me with stories and photos of her adventures and I was hooked.

Our family which consisted of me, my three brothers and mum and dad had just moved to New Zealand having lived in Fiji and the Solomon Islands for almost five years. The family was soon to move to the high country of New Zealand just below the Southern Alps where skiing was readily accessible. I became quite obsessed with the idea of skiing and I just happened to fit my aunt's leather ski boots. (I was living with her as I was something of a problem child and sometimes mum needed a break from looking after four boys.)

My aunt was a serious gardener so she offered me the opportunity of owning the ski boots if I would produce many hours of hard labour in her garden - something our family traditionally called a "bob a job". When we shifted to the Alps I found to my dismay that leather ski boots had gone out of fashion a little while beforehand. Bugger!

It did not deter me from hitting the slopes with or without my leather ski boots. So my oldest brother Danny, who had just got his license, and I drove to Round Hill ski field at Lake Tekapo to try our feet at skiing for the very first time.

There are very few defining moments in life that you know will change things forever: first kiss, first love, first job, first car and the like but that day's skiing was one of mine. I still remember the fear, the rush and looking back how stupid I was not taking a lesson. I remember it as well as the day I had skiing today at Chamonix. I remember how awe-inspiring it felt afterwards and the stories I told to my friends when I excitedly got back to school the next day. I just loved how skiing made me feel and continues to do so.

There are also few things that you dream about in life that do actually exceed your expectations as skiing for me is very close to living your dreams. The feeling never dies and after 35 years of skiing all over the world I would like to share my thoughts on it.

"When I ski I get a feeling of forever and a feeling of not wanting to stop. I feel like I am floating and almost weightless. Most of all, I feel like I am a river flowing and like a bird flying".
Rebecca Solo, Blind competitive skier

In my high school years, after skiing for a while, I got a job at the nearest ski-field working in ski hire and on the lifts at Lake Ohau so I could afford to ski more. In my last year I worked at the bottom of the ski field at the Ski Lodge. At high school I would manage the Friday night cinema club and would often show Warren Miller ski films or other movies like James Bond which had phenomenal ski moments in them.

I was also in the school and Ohau ski teams and we would compete against other schools and ski-field teams throughout the South Island even though we were always out-classed by individuals that had started skiing not long after they learnt to walk. The Twizel High School ski team would turn up at what we would consider very up-market resorts and be the laughing stock of the ski race - we looked like the Jamaican bob sled team in the movie Cool Runnings. None of us could afford new or even close to new ski equipment or clothes and just made do with what we could afford.

Nearly every season since school I have bought a season pass and skied every weekend and holiday possible throughout New Zealand where we have some fantastic skiing and many mountains that are only reachable by helicopter or a very long ski tour. Can you image how good it feels you join some friends and share a helicopter ride through the Alps until you find a remote mountain covered in fresh snow and ski it all to yourself, all day? Heaven!

Anyway I loved both the skiing and the après from an early age and that has not changed a bit. I can tell you in all sincerity that this love of skiing never dies; the urge just gets stronger and stronger, something I can't say about many other sports or pastimes. There are too many sports which are short lived due to ageing. Every day you bump into people who say I used to do that or this but that was a while ago now so they sit glued to the television or a DVD reliving a few of those glorious moments they once had in whatever sport they once participated in. In skiing those celebrated moments happen throughout every day and it's never too late to start or re-start. So get off that couch you lazy fat bastard and find out where the closest ski-field is to you and give it a whirl. I promise you that you will not be disappointed. If you are, imagine my concern!

"When it comes to skiing there's a difference between what you thinks it's going to be like, what it's going to be like and what you tell your friends it was like."
Anonymous

There have many, many trends in the sport and the introduction of snowboarding meant a whole new generation was attracted to the slopes. This increase in demand for the sport has meant new resorts have opened and the need for existing resorts to improve all round facilities. Some trends died a slow death such as Mono boarding (although there are still a few enthusiasts around that would dispute that, especially in Chamonix home to the Mono-board museum in Le Rencard restaurant and bar in Argentiere). The skiing industry has seen some massive changes during the 35 years I have skied and technology has played a key role in making it more accessible to everyone. This technology has given skiers the edge to become advanced skiers in a much shorter time span.

Skiing has always been highly technological, from its primitive origin until today. The oldest skis were found in Russia dating back to 6,300 BC. I have visited the ski museum in Oslo Norway and it is fascinating to see the historical progression of a means of transport to the recreational activity and sport it is today. You will find the ski museum underneath the Olympic ski jump which is a must walk to the top unless you suffer from vertigo.

"I remember feeling that technology was like trying to draw with your boot. In a ski boot. It was the most indirect way to work imaginable, but the potential had us all excited. I started in stop motion."
Chris Wedge

In the excellent book by Roland Huntford Two Planks and a Passion, which tells the dramatic history of skiing, he depicts how skiing was invented in the ice ages 20,000 years ago; the first recorded ski race was on 30th March 1843 in Tromso Norway; in 1898-99 an Englishman Dr Henry Lunn organised for a group of skiers to go Chamonix for the first known package ski holiday.

Lunn was to have tremendous success bringing the British skier to the Alps topping over 5000 skiers per season. This helped develop Chamonix as well as other resorts such as Adleboden and Wegen in Switzerland. To him is ultimately due credit for the modern winter sports industry.

The world's first ski resort was Davos in Switzerland which was followed by St Moritz and Chamonix was soon to follow but for a long time mountaineering was dominant and deeply antagonist towards skiers. The first ski school was opened by Johann Schneider in St Anton in 1911-12 and paved the way for mass ski tourism. On 14th December 1911 Amundsen and his party, who saw themselves not as explorers but as skiers, reached the South Pole with Captain Robert Scott's expedition 300 miles behind because of their lack of skiing skills. In 1928 Austria was the first country in the world to officially recognise ski instructors, the test and syllabus.

"There is a simple explanation for the evolution of alpine skiing in the last two decades of the nineteenth century. The classic age of mountaineering ended around 1870, by which time the great summits had been climbed. The ski offered something new. It removed the last vestige of fear from the mountain world".
Roland Huntford, Two Planks and a Passion

I look back over the last 35 years with an abundance of gratitude as few people have been as lucky as I have to have had as much skiing and the incomparable lifestyle and alpine experience that are associated with it. Even though life has often tried to get the better of me, skiing continues to inspire me and rescue me from a world of chaos. There are few sports or even activities in life where you can get away to another world that is full of pure escapism, but to a place that is more real than our world that is filled with pollution, war, greed, corruption, putrescence, narrow-mindedness, pettiness, hate, cruelty, obesity, sickness, starvation, racial and religious intolerance, dishonesty, crime, overpopulation and poverty.

Skiing is a sensation that is difficult to describe. Those of us who know the sensation like me wish that every person could be lucky enough to have a chance to experience it but few do. No matter how hard I try to describe the sensation, no matter how much you hear about it, no matter how many ski movies I watch, no matter how much I ski, nothing can provide the slightest inkling of the sensation. When you ski it's like stepping through the wardrobe in the C.S. Lewis novels as you step into the most perfect and natural world you will ever see. It's also comparable to when you deep sea dive as there is nothing but you and miles and miles of ocean and a feeling of elation and euphoria.

"Skiing is a wonderful metaphor for life."
Robert Redford

I have met thousands of fascinating people over the years skiing even if it is just for a few minutes on a T-bar, chair lift, cable car, snow-train or gondola, and have made many lifelong friends through the sport. Skiing can be an unbelievably social sport or the total opposite as it is the idyllic sport to do on your own. Skiing teaches you to enjoy your own companionship and increases your independence. Skiing brings all walks of life together on common ground and brings out the very best in human nature.

You arrive at a ski resort and suddenly you have a few thousand new friends that you share a mutual interest with and most often a common goal. Après ski is almost as famous as skiing itself as the sport provides the pluperfect platform to socialise and to easily converge with other like minded people. For me it's also the most romantic of sports, the breathtaking Alps, a roaring log fire, drinking champagne, a hot Jacuzzi, a local hearty mountain meal, red wine, the magic of snow falling are all unblemished joys to share with a loved one. I adore seeing old couples ski, those who have unmistakably been skiing together for many years; it's very inspirational and you are never too old to start. I have heard many stories of people learning late in life such as one instructor teaching a woman aged 64 who skied well into her late 80s.

It is a well known fact that people that ski together stay together and there is way less divorce rate amongst serious skiers; ha but a higher possibility that your partner will run off with a ski instructor if you don't ski as well.

My cousin Rose enrolled in a ski instructor's course some years before I did and fell in love with her examiner Todd. She married him and they are one of the happiest couples you could ever meet - she even makes him ski on his day off!

It's a super healthy sport as you do it, but it also motivates you to get fit in preparation and we all know the benefits of exercise. People spend a fortune going to health spas, retreats and outdoor rehabilitation centres with the majority of patients being totally un-rehabilitated and going back to the old routine. The National Health Service and other international medical and mental health institutions would have far better results by sending their patients on ski holidays.

I had a very good friend who was a sublime snowboarder and skateboarder. He would often challenge me to a top to bottom downhill race on his snowboard and would sometimes beat me to the bottom by not turning at all. James had a problem with drugs and alcohol and after checking out of rehabilitation soon committed suicide. He loved the mountains and if only he had revisited them I am sure he would be alive today.

For me skiing comes with the continuous lure of adventure which I have always desired but as much as anything a means of self-discovery. It provides me with a new escapade every day and is an ideal way to forget about your past problems in life and set them to rest. It's very cathartic. Being on the mountain you are so far removed from society that literally all you can hear is your skis turning. It's the unsurpassed form of escapism in the world but really, is it escapism or the purest form of reality there is?

It's as close as you will ever get to whatever your understanding of god is that's for sure. In my book there's nothing superior to the anticipation of the thrills that you know lie in store for you before a day's skiing.

"If you aren't crashing you aren't skiing."
Well-known ski instructing term.

Teaching skiing is very satisfying and it feels wonderful contributing and giving something back to a sport that has given me so much. I don't care if you are qualified to teach or not, if you are a better skier than the person you are skiing with I am sure there is something that you can pass on to give them a hand. The more you ski the better you get and the better you get the more you enjoy the sport, it's as simple as that. And although age affects your physical ability to perform it doesn't affect your ski technique or ability to progress along the learning curve. I met my ski racing hero Franz Klammer (1976 Olympic downhill gold medal winner and winner of 25 world cup down-hills) at a golf tournament in Monaco a few years ago and he is still one of the fittest, most vibrant and healthiest looking men I have ever met and he is close to 60 years old. Ski technology has made skiing assessable to anyone. I have taught hundreds of people to ski over the years and most of them are still doing it on a regular basis to this day.

Unfortunately many of my friends who were once super keen skiers have let daily life and its responsibilities take over and their routine no longer allows time to hit the slopes. If only they knew what they were missing. It is unfortunate that many ski instructors lose their passion for skiing too, becoming complacent, obnoxious and dispassionate which is reflected in how they communicate. I witness this everywhere I ski and the best ski instructor is a happy one and to the rest of them I'd say love it or leave it or take a break from it and renew that passion that you know is there.

"Faster, faster until the thrill of speed overcomes the fear of death."
Anon

Skiing is also about controlling your fear and testing no one else's limits but your own and thus is very personal. I have clocked 153 km at Turoa ski field in New Zealand skiing down a glacier through a speed trap where your time is calculated. I skied on a pair of 234cm Élan speed skis and it's the optimum way to test your fear. I was heavier than the other skiers who were clocking over 160km but fear and your subconscious is something that is hard to control. The world speed record on skis is 251.4 km or 156 mph held by Simon Origone. Speed skiers regularly break the 200km barrier which is faster than terminal velocity and something I am aspiring to do. The better at skiing you get the less fear you have and this new found confidence often hides in your subconscious, this is disputable whether this is a good thing or not due to the increased level of risk.

Sometimes you wonder if your time is up when you are on a vertical slope that will kill you if you don't keep turning or when you have been pushing yourself for so long without serious injury that your respect for the mountain somehow vanishes and fear dissipates.

"When you back off, it's easier to make mistakes. For me it's better to ski fast."
Bode Miller

Skiing throws you into the arms of mother-nature and experiencing oneness with the natural world. You realise in the mountains just how insignificant you really are in the scheme of things and thus it gives you an appreciation of life found not only there but in relation to everything else. Skiing is a first-rate way to travel and discover the world in all its beauty by reconnecting your body, mind and spirit.

But above all skiing provides you with an elated sensation, a thrilling feeling of complete euphoria as the gravitational pull self contains and stimulates you tenfold. It's all about finding that balance between flow and resistance. Nothing has made me feel as exhilarated or as overwhelmingly alive as skiing. Sure there are comparative sports for adrenalin seekers but none offer the complete alpine experience that skiing does. It makes you a factory for producing endorphins and the more you produce the more you want.

It's also a well-known fact that endorphins make you feel blissful and give you a natural high superior to anything an artificial one can give you. Stress dampens our spirits, it suppresses our joy. Adrenalin gets rid of stress and renews us.

We often think of fun activities as things we work to deserve rather than something we have the right to experience. We too rarely think of fun as essential to our health and well being. We are governed by what we are taught in schools, universities, tradition, society's standards and expectations which all consider pleasure and recreation something to be earned. Bullshit!

In Chamonix I rappelled down treacherous leaches, skied dangerous couloirs, gravitated on 40 degree north faces, jumped cliff lines and the like and if I have not got you hooked by now I never will.

"Life shrinks or expands in proportion to one's courage."
Anais Nin

Five years ago after having spent literally thousands of days on snow I thought I was the best skier on the planet and yes skiing can also be very egotistical. Just look how quickly fashion changes in ski wear and equipment. Skiing fashion has progressed from elegance and class from its first origins, peaking with outrageous multicoloured monstrosities in the eighties before finding a better balance now.

I must confess that I did wear a nice one piece throughout the eighties with black, yellow, orange and lime; yuck talk about being a fashion victim. Technology is playing an important part as ski clothes are getting lighter but stronger with the likes of leading brands like Arc'terycx, Northface, Salomon or Icebreaker for instance. You do however have to commend the snowboarders fashion labels as their fashion trends progress much quicker than skiing and perhaps that's due to the younger crowd it generally attracts or the rapid growth of the sport.

I have regularly changed my ski gear to keep up with technology and of course fashion. Like numerous skiers who have skied for years, I was of the point of view that a few years ago my skiing had somewhat peaked. Well that was until I enrolled in a season long ski instructing course. There were seven of us from a variety of backgrounds and age groups. It was soon evident that I had had as many days on the mountain as the group combined but it was a little harder to teach an old dog new tricks - when it came to the first exam they all passed and I failed. It was one of the most embarrassing days of my life especially as I failed on my wedge turn (and the examiners had also booked out my restaurant and bar in the Alps to hold the awards evening). The wedge turn is also known as a snow plough or pizza and is a very important turn to teach as it sets up the basic position you will use forever and a day.

Well that was the optimal event that has recently happened to my skiing and I gained a new and deeper respect for the sport I had treasured for the previous 30 years as a result. It has helped me write this book and I have found a deeper love and understanding of skiing but most importantly I enjoy it more on a fresher level and I have never looked back.

As I have learnt new methods and techniques I cannot begin to tell you how much more I started to enjoy skiing, more than I thought possible. I had always prided myself on being one of the fastest skiers on the mountain as I love the rush speed gives you and I have always lacked fear; but now I was being taught how to ski as fast as I wanted by carving, railing and edging in total control. I learnt about how the new technology affects the performance of the ski and how to fully utilise that by applying certain techniques. I learnt to ski contrasting types of skis on different terrain and in diverse conditions. It was like a whole new world had opened up to me. I re-sat my exams and passed at top of the class and have taken many courses and lessons since and still do on a regular basis. I encourage anyone who skis, no matter what their, level to take lessons as there is always something new to learn.

> **"Gotta use your brain, it's the most important part of your equipment."**
> **Kevin Andrews and Warren Miller**

And that is what leads me back to Chamonix as one area of skiing I still wanted to conquer was off piste and powder snow. I had done a little heli-skiing and some ski touring in New Zealand. I had skied many powder days but I was not satisfied with either my ability in such snow or the amount I had skied. I had previously skied way off piste in St Anton in Austria with friends and a guide. I was hooked and wanted more. All experienced skiers do.

I have explained in some detail why I was attracted to Chamonix so let me explain the skiing here and you will probably be on the next plane too. My first few days on the mountain were like learning to ski again as the snow was very deep and initially hard to turn in with the amount of freedom and movement I am used to. I was clearly out of my depth and after a couple of nasty falls in deep powder I was almost ready to pack my bags. Instead I got a lesson - then I was off and never looked back.

Although the basic body position does not change that much in fresh snow the movement is more exaggerated and definitely more physical. Without a doubt you have to push your boundaries further but the sensation you feel is quadrupled in comparison to on piste skiing.

I have a friend, Grant Kevey, who is one of New Zealand's most knowledgeable and well-versed skiers and who I had skied with at St Anton, Austria. We argued the merits of both styles as I was previously hooked on piste skiing - namely long fast giant slalom type turns, where the thrill comes from edging and speed. Nowadays the only time Grant ever skied on piste was when he was on his way to ski off piste. He also believes that off piste skiing is much better on your body and limbs than piste skiing but that you do have to maintain a high level of fitness to fully enjoy both.

Many experienced piste skiers suffer from bad knees when they get over 50 and have to give up where as Grant believes he will never have these problems. It is true that many once regular skiers give up the sport due to physical problems caused by too much skiing. Grant's passion did rub off on me and also motivated me to find out for myself.

The day I skied off piste with Grant, his wife Joya, a guide and some friends in St Anton, it started with a one and a half hour climb once we had taken the very last chairlift to the top of the highest peak. We then skied in some magic fresh deep powder snow for what seemed like miles and miles. Out of nowhere a taxi van picked us up at the very bottom and drove us back to the lifts. We then caught the telecabin to the highest point of St Anton which involves getting in a very small gondola to the peak. You then have to ski the steepest terrain found anywhere on the entire mountain and out through a stunning valley. I was skiing on a brand new pair of 180cm Volkl Race Tigers Giant Slalom skis and it was a lesson to be learnt in choosing the right skis to match the conditions and type of snow you were skiing in. I could hardly walk the next day and when I skied every turn was like being punched in the leg by George Foreman.

I have since realised that switching to a wide off piste ski makes it a million times easier to confidently ski any of the off piste conditions. Every ski has its place and you need to make the right decision in choosing the ski to suit not only your ability but also the conditions. I promise it will make a monolithic difference to the enjoyment of your skiing.

"*There's no waiting for friends on a powder day.*"
Anon

At the very beginning of the season in Chamonix I found a brilliant boutique ski shop only metres across the road from the historic church in Argentiere called Namaste. It is owned and managed by Rob who came out for a season from Sweden about twenty years ago, fell in love with Chamonix and never left. The shop always smelt of hot burning ski wax, the sound of skis being tuned and Rob's gorgeous black dog was always up for a cuddle. Namaste had every type of ski you could imagine including cross country and touring. I was able to swap my skis as often as I liked and by the end of the season I had tried half a dozen different skis all with a different speciality that I had never skied on before. The skis were always finely tuned and waxed which gave me that added confidence to ski hard and fast on them.

Namaste was right next door to the chalet Le Marti but they no longer used the shop for ski hire. When I asked why, Rob told me that he was not prepared to offer companies the outrageous commission they were asking. When I delved into this a little more I found that many businesses offered commission kickbacks and that it can make a sizeable difference to your business's bottom line. A chalet business will get kickbacks from ski hire, lift tickets, restaurant bookings and even other accommodation.

Chamonix offers such a stupendous variety of off piste skiing due to the multiple landscapes in the valley that they publish an off piste guide book which gives you a choice of 12 to 20 different printed runs you can do on every one of the five ski fields in the valley. There are obviously hundreds more off piste runs on each ski field but it is made quite clear you enter at your own risk.

There are five ski fields in the Chamonix Valley and you have a choice of downhill skiing, snowboarding, telemark, free riding, freestyle, snow park, speed riding, ski touring, cross country and of course off piste!

Each ski field was owned individually by a family that originally farmed the land. It was only recently that they amalgamated and the Compagnie du Mont Blanc was formed. The company now owns them all apart from Les Houches. Your Chamonix unlimited ski pass is able to be used in each of the five ski fields. I am told by many of people that have skied here for many years that the amalgamation has meant the mountains are way less competitive than they used to be. Time was when they would open earlier and close later and glaciers were even open in the summer.

I was shocked at some of the facilities such as very old chairlifts that you can walk faster than but there is a high speed lift on each ski field. However that does not detract from the stupendous skiing here but you would get more turns in with new high speed lifts.

This book is in no way intended to be a ski guide, but I will touch briefly on what I enjoyed over the season. My first day was at Brevant which has sensational views as it faces Mont Blanc. In the later months of the season Brevant basks in the sun and you can enjoy the very best of spring skiing. I found the skiing here to be average in comparison to the other fields. However I would often take the Brevant gondola to the top just for the view and the panoramic restaurant – it's worth eating all their cheese filled dishes just for the view.

My best day there was without a doubt Christmas Day when I skied in to the abyss. I also enjoyed drinking Heineken while listening to DJs from Le Verte playing to trendy crowds on sunny spring afternoons. From Brevant you can take the cable car across to Flegere which has some excellent off piste runs and some very steep vertical. It also commands stunning views of Mont Blanc and the surrounding peaks. It has one high speed chair lift but the other four are a joke and the slowest and most frustrating I have ever ridden on. There is nothing worse than having a brilliant ski run and then having to get on a pedestrian ski lift. There are way too many slow and old ski lifts in the Chamonix area and as they must be making a fortune every year so I do not see any reason why they should not upgrade. It was my biggest gripe by far especially as all its main and even less well known competitors have much amended facilities.

The first day I skied Flegere with Matt Whitaker and Johnny another experienced New Zealand skier, I had two terrific falls in waste deep powder and almost snapped a leg. It was a timely reminder in knowing that there was going to be a lot to learn in perfecting my off piste skiing. Flegere also has one of the most scenic chairlift rides with stunning views of Mont Blanc to your left and other souring peaks such as Les Drus.

"Gravity is love and every turn a leap of faith."
Anon

Across the valley from Flegere is my pick of the bunch in the Chamonix valley and where I spent the most time by far, and for good reason, as the Grand Montets offers some of the best off piste skiing found anywhere in the world and is famous globally as a result. It is a mountainous mythical place and offers the experienced skier a stupendous variety of long and very steep off piste runs.

The facilities are not too bad as well with a high speed six seater chair lift, a telecabin to 3,300 meters and another to 2,700 meters. I can now happily say that I have had some of the best skiing in my life on Grand Montets which includes dozens of powder days with few people around to spoil my fun. As it was only a five minute walk from Gite le Belvédère where I stayed later on in the season I was often making first tracks. It was also very social as you would often catch up and ski with my new found friends.

La Tour is the last ski field in the valley and the village is around 1,400 meters above sea level. Although the mountain is quite gentle and thus family friendly I loved the skiing here. It is wide and open on one side and filled with trees on the other where you can ski all the way to Vallorcine which is only a few kilometres from the Swiss border. Tree line skiing in New Zealand is something we lack, so I made the most of it. I had some wonderful powder days at Le Tour and as the hardcore skiers were often elsewhere, it came with the bonus of being quiet.

Les Houches is similar to Le Tour but a lot more famous due to the fact that they have held a world cup downhill ski race there every year since 1948. Les Houches is best suited for learners and one of the reasons it's so popular with families. It wasn't part of my motivation for coming to Chamonix but it is stunningly beautiful. You ski right beneath Mont Blanc and through trees and forests – it's a great place to take a break from the other slopes. The highlight of skiing Les Houches is without a doubt taking on the Kandahar downhill run. Best skied later in the season – when there are less people the faster you can go and the safer it is. "Oh Yeah".

Here are a few of the memorable runs I tried that I found through looking at the natives.co.uk ski guide. The Italian Bowl - take Telesiege de la Herse, cut left at the top and follow the cliff face. It opens out into a superb pitch where the snow holds up well. The Canadian Bowl -take the Bochard bubble, cut back under the lift and traverse. Drop down, aiming for the peak to the left of the bubble, keeping your speed up as you'll need to go uphill. You can get into the bowl on the right or left of the peak. Combe de la Pendant - Bochard to the top, drop past the kit-on area and traverse high to your left. Again your options are limitless here. Just enjoy! Pas de Chevre - dropping down from the top of Grands Montets onto the Vallée Blanche, four long, steep couloirs. From right to left, and in increasing order of steepness: Le Pas de Chevre, Couloir Centrale, Couloir Rectiligne and, strictly for the hardcore, Couloir des Drus.

There are also literally thousands of other off piste ski runs with the most famous being the Vallée Blanche, the White Valley. I started this book in the Vallée Blanche as it is without a doubt the icing on a very well made cake in Chamonix, it attracts thousands of extra skiers to the area every year, even if the skiing isn't the best. The route is about 20km long and starts at the Aiguille du Midi station at 3842 metres and can be skied by intermediate to advanced skiers depending on the route. You can finish either at the Montenvers railway station or in Chamonix itself depending on snow conditions. When you finish at the Montenvers railway station you do however get to witness firsthand the devastating effect global warming is having – you have to walk up a couple of hundred metres of steps where the glacier has receded.

It gives you around 2,800 meters of vertical skiing but the highlight is not the skiing itself but the breathtaking, heart stopping scenery. There are points where you feel encapsulated in a giant abyss of pure white as far as the eye can see. It's like when you are far out at sea and it is dead calm and all you can see is water. The hardest part of the Vallée Blanche is even before you put your skis on as you have to walk down the famously precipitous arête. There is a safety rope to help guide you which I clung on to like there was no tomorrow. The walk which takes about 15 minutes is not for the faint hearted and I personally found it scary as all hell even with crampons on my ski boots.

There are numerous deaths every year on this small decent as people do slip and fall over the edge which is only feet away from the path cut through ice and snow. On one side there is a 2000 meter vertical drop and one slip is all it takes. Only a few years ago someone put on their skis without knowing or finding out about the conditions and skied to her death as she fell 1000 metres in front of a crowd of people.

My advice is don't attempt it without crampons and if you are inexperienced I would recommend clipping your harness to the safety rope. As well as complete safety kit of transceiver, harness, ropes, probe and shovel you also need extra warm clothes, a survival blanket and food in your pack so that if you are one of the unlucky ones and you fall down one of the hundreds of crevasses you don't die of hypothermia and you can keep your energy levels up by eating. You also shouldn't attempt it without a guide or extremely knowledgeable local skier, but once you have got yourself organised a trip through the Vallée Blanche is a memory that will stay with you forever- it's the stuff that allegories and legends are made of.

The Star That Fell to Earth

On a cold, late November day in 1955 Louis Lachenal, the first Frenchman to stand on the summit of an 8000 meter peak, was casting about Chamonix for a partner to ski with him on the Vallée Blanche. He met up with experienced guide Jean-Pierre Payot and they took the cable car to the Aiguille du Midi. Payot recalls the day "We skied a steep couloir to reach the start of the Vallée

Blanche, chatting calmly to each other. It was quite cold and the wind was getting up. We arrived at the first seracs, the wind was directly in our faces, we didn't have glasses back then and we were skiing unroped. Louis commented that the strong wind was dangerous. I was barely 2 meters ahead. I hardly had time to turn when I heard his aluminium skis scrape across the ice as he fell into the crevasse." Louis Lachenal had broken through a snow bridge, 25 meters below, the back of his head struck a block of ice and snapped his neck, he must have died instantly. Payot shouted below but there was no reply. In a supreme effort he climbed back to the cable car station which was now closed, he then climbed on to a refuge and telephoned for help. It was now 11pm and the guides in Chamonix were not keen to turn out. Only Lachenal's friends were prepared to come, although they were later joined by guides. They lit tires above the crevasse to keep warm and one of them descended to recover the body of the great alpinist. At 11am the next day they arrived back in Chamonix. Louis Lachenal is buried in Chamonix cemetery.

A few weeks before I skied the Vallée Blanche exactly that did happen. A tourist was skiing with a highly experienced guide and when you are repeatedly told to ski directly behind your guide you really should do so. The skier was having fun making his own tracks, as we all do, but unfortunately he skied into a crevasse - one of hundreds you will see when skiing here - and to his death.

What is also tremendous about Chamonix is its location on both the Swiss and Italian borders. Verbier, another of the world's top ski resorts is just under an hour away by car and Cormayeur in Italy is only 11.6km by driving through the Mont Blanc tunnel. While Cormayeur is comparable to Les Houches or Le Tour, Verbier is an outstanding and very large resort, taking you to the same height as Grand Montets at 3,300 meters.

The view at the top of Verbier is one of the most spectacular you will ever see - the full panorama of the Swiss, Italian and French Alps. Verbier is also gigantic and there is skiing to appeal to skiers of every level, especially advanced. I loved it and the upmarket ski village is almost 100% wooden made as opposed to Chamonix where there are plenty of old concrete structures.

Verbier is a very upscale Swiss resort but French speaking and comes with a price tag to match and mainly appeals to rich British but also attracts a very affluent international clientele. The small village centre is only a couple of streets but they are full of trendy bars, restaurants and plenty of elite nightclubs where many spend a small fortune. The skiing here is world class and I rate it as one of the world's top ten ski resorts. It is absolutely mammoth: you can ski all day just getting from one end to the other. It is funny that often when I heard Verbier mentioned it would always be followed with did you know Richard Branson has a Chalet there, who gives a toss if he has a chalet there or not, certainly it should only be his concern, it doesn't make the skiing any better that's for sure. Verbier is a favourite resort of many competitive skiers and successful British Olympic skier Chemmy Alcott told me it was easily her favourite resort. Chemmy is easily the United Kingdom's answer to Lindsay Von.

> ***"Standing at the start gate, adrenalin pumping – concentrate the mind, focus the body – GO! GO! GO!"***
> **Chemmy Alcott**

There are lots of resorts throughout Europe that market and promote themselves not according to the fantastic alpine terrain, but who goes there. Its' a very insecure world sometimes isn't it? On the other hand there are some famous ski resorts such as Gstaad in Switzerland which is a small village with three five star hotels and a timeless reputation for exclusivity. It's the sort of place where real royalty goes and where discretion counts above all else. Then the likes of Paris Hilton turn up and suddenly a once well preserved culture and status is reduced to the equivalent of Hello Magazine.

Courmayeur is a must visit as it is a very traditional Italian mountain and you will soon be caught up in its authentic hospitality, excellent restaurants and bars. The skiing is good fun, there are plenty of trees and you get to see Mount Blanc from the other side. Although I get a little bored with the skiing there, it is nevertheless a leisurely way to spend a day especially skiing through the trees. The village is also very appealing and most of the bars offer free anti pasta and entertainment for après ski. The greatest thing about it though is its proximity to Chamonix and if you want a break from the brusqueness of the French this is the place to come for the Italian antidote - the restaurants are superb and the overall standard of food competitive with its French neighbours. The Italians do cheap food better than the French, end of story and the high end of the market is a different kettle of fish altogether.

I would also like to touch on the other skiing in Chamonix. Thousands of people come to Chamonix as it offers some of the world's best and most extreme ski touring. Ski touring is simply skiing areas where there are no lifts and offers a freedom that cannot be found on the commercial fields. It is a rapidly growing sport as nature tourism takes off. Over the ski season I was to meet hundreds of ski touring enthusiasts and most of them were advanced skiers who had changed from piste skiing to off piste ski touring. It seemed like a natural progression to ski tour and also signified a deeper respect and understanding of the mountain surroundings and its dangers.

Unlike other European ski resorts you cannot start your ski tour in France by being dropped off by a helicopter. Heli-skiing is totally banned due to rules about helicopter landings on mountains which are often designated national parks. However because of Chamonix's proximity to the Italian and Swiss boarders you can easily be dropped off in another country and in some instances ski back to France.

To ski tour you basically have to start again as far as your equipment is concerned. Ski touring gear is lighter and more suited to off piste terrain. To start you will need touring skis and touring bindings. Then you will need ski touring boots which are lighter and designed to be easier to walk in and to skin-up with your skis on. As ski touring is exceptionally dangerous you undoubtedly need the complete collection of safety kit I mentioned earlier. It doesn't come cheap however, my brother Peter got hooked on ski touring and all his new equipment cost around five thousand Swiss Francs.

Chamonix offers thousands of ski touring options but the most famous is the Haute Route - a five to seven day tour from Chamonix to Zermatt in Switzerland. The route was first made by a local Chamonix doctor, Dr Payot in 1903. I met a young American man Jason McKnight, who was planning to do the whole trip by himself, but using 1940s ski gear and equipment. He was also going to attempt the tour with no GPS or Altimeter which are essential parts of safety equipment in these modern times. His skis were Tua Grand Montets long boards and certainly not the shaped type. His binding was a three pin and cable rarely seen nowadays and the boots were leather like Frankenstein – in fact they looked exactly the same as the ones I had earned from my aunt 35 years previously.

He used skins to climb the big cols on the Haute Route and he emailed me and said he did not die coming down the spine-breaking couloirs that were life changing stuff. He also added (do not try at home)!

All the biggest names in skiing have skied Chamonix at one point or another and while I was there Seth Morrison was making a movie with his company Teton Gravity Research – the number one extreme ski movie making company in the world. Seth has been repeatedly voted the world's number one free skier and you only need to take a look at any of his ski movies to see why. Not only does Seth ski the hardest vertical runs found anywhere in the world he jumps them at the same time and seeing is believing with this guy.

There are a bunch of others such as Californian Glen Plake who bought a house in Chamonix. Glen is almost as famous for his long Mohawk hair style as he is for his extreme skiing. When asked what he loved about the skiing at Chamonix so much his reply was: "Things can happen in Chamonix that can't happen anywhere else you know? There's never a bad day in Chamonix. Dreams should definitely come true here for sure." Glen skied in the cult eighties ski film The Blizzard of AAHHH's a movie that went a long way to helping confirm the legendary extreme skiing status that Chamonix now prides itself on. The film starts off like this. "The American ski industry afraid of huge law suits and burdened by insurance rates that are criminal does not promote believable ski heroes because believable ski heroes are the ones that ski the extreme." It's a must see ski movie.

Sponsoring extreme skiing has become big business as well as having a sizeable impact on the dangerous side of skiing. These ruthless sponsors push and push people to the limits and often to their deaths. There is much debate about this in Chamonix and there is one argument that sponsors are aiding and abetting people to kill themselves and the other argument is that the funding and latest equipment means people are better equipped and safer than they might have been without the sponsorship.

All of the big snow associated sports brands have people in Chamonix who are just there to ski, enter competitions, do photography, fashion and video shoots as well as test their sponsor's latest equipment. There are also many accomplished skiers that are on the verge of becoming professional and even skiers like 60 year old Mark Courville who are walking ambassadors for the brand and thus given free ski or snow board equipment each year.

I found the competitive spirit amongst people in Chamonix, especially between men and woman, engrossing. I found that woman celebrate what they have overcome in skiing whilst the men often take a "my dicks bigger than yours" perspective. You often hear competitive conversations out socially that are centred around who has skied the hardest extreme run while putting down their fellow skiers' efforts. These people are losing site of the joy of skiing as it lies with what you achieve personally. Certainly there is a certain amount of egotism associated with being at the top of any sport but bragging and boasting about it is nothing more than an insecurity reflex.

I met many ski instructors over the season including numerous instructors from the Ecole du Ski Chamonix, where once again you have to be born in the valley to become an instructor. Their oldest instructors are in their seventies and are still having a ball and really do add to the delightful atmosphere of the mountain spirit. There are other ski instructor companies that cater 100% to the English speaking market. It's worth bearing in mind that when you sit your ski instructors exams at the Ecole du Ski you have to be within 100th of a second to a world qualifying giant slalom race time! They stand out in their all red ski outfits and I always enjoyed watching them ski with such obvious skill and expertise especially off piste. Once a year they all get together, about 200 of them and ski down the ski slope in town carrying a live flame, it looks spectacular on the snow. It looks like the ski-field is on fire from a distance and is a photographer's dream. They then consume gallons of hot mulled wine and party late into the evening.

I talked to lots of ski instructors about my book as I was interested in talking about ski teaching trends, what people expected to learn skiing in Chamonix and where they thought skiing was heading. Since the arrival of shaped skis in 1993 skiing has changed not only when it comes to gear but also the way it is taught. I interviewed one of the best skiers I could find who happened to be a 36 year old Englishman with his own boutique style ski school. I saw Mark Gear ski a couple of times and he was as good as anyone I have ever watched. Mark is originally from Essex and learnt to ski on a dry slope where he fell in love with the sport. He soon became a dry slope instructor. His love of skiing brought him to Chamonix when he was 21. He did all sorts of jobs, like many people do here, to support himself, and to keep skiing. It took him five years of hard work to pass the British Association of Ski Instructors (BASS) level four exams (there are only 270 qualified grade four instructors in the world).

When he finally became an instructor he worked for Evolution Two another renowned ski school for a few years and then set up his business, All Mountain Performance. What really interested me was that Mark's company only gave lessons to intermediate and advanced skiers as the majority of skiers that come to Chamonix fit into this category.

Most of his clients also skied on average three to five weeks a year and many chose All Mountain Performance because they could learn to ski off piste confidently while maintaining balance and control. Firstly, Mark made it quite clear that technology had made skiing much easier for every skier while applying new techniques to his clients with terms he uses such as pivot and rotating, spin and slash, while holding the edge with perfect control. This was especially the case on the big fat skis we see today. "We also encourage our regular skiers to get fit before they come to ski and it is clearly evident that the ones that do have a much more enjoyable time," he said.

Mark also said All Mountain Performance's ethos was all about teaching control and versatility so that clients can then express themselves with snow and in any terrain. As off piste skiing is way more adventurous Mark would take the majority of his clients through untouched terrain with a 100% I want to do that again ratio.

Mark has skied in all the top resorts all over Europe, but loves Chamonix above all else for its big vertical drops, its steepness and variety of terrain. His objective with his customers was to find the balance between flow and resistance creating an everlasting and memorable ski lesson. "Chamonix is also a great place to live all year round". It sure is now for Mark as half way through the interview his wife won 40,000 Euros on a French television game show.

My advice to beginners is always take lessons and for those wanting to improve their skiing, take as many lessons as they can afford as there is always something new to learn. If you can't afford lessons you can't afford to ski in my book but read as much as you can or watch ski DVDs, which I would always recommend before anyone hits the slopes. And that goes for even the most advanced skier as well. I highly recommend video analysis as not only is it fun to watch yourself ski but also a great way to improve.

Ski with gear that is up to date, it doesn't have to be the latest and most expensive but it should be no older than ten years. Comfortable boots are paramount and I highly recommend foot beds. If you are buying new ski boots find a specialist boot fitter. Always have warm clothing as you will not enjoy your skiing when you are cold. New Zealand makes the best winter clothing in the world from merino wool: the label is called Icebreaker and I have used it for under-layers for over 15 years and never been freezing cold. I also always buy Gortex and as a result never get wet but there are many other brands that are now as good. It's just not much fun skiing cold.

During the season I skied on a variety of different types of skis and each time the sensation was different and I had to alter my technique and stance to improve. Repetition is the key to succeeding in any field and I often take people I am teaching to a slope that suits their ability and get them to ski it again and again until they get it absolutely right. When they start to get a little bored with the routine I then ask them to really push and they soon notice changes and improvements.

When teaching skiing I have had to deal with all levels of fear and I found this to be a regular occurrence in Chamonix. I would like to be brave and say I have little fear on the mountain but when you come close to death your natural instincts kick into gear and there is nothing but fear. I felt I lacked fear until I skied Chamonix and it has made me appreciate that fear comes to all of us but the more we practise in extreme conditions the smaller it becomes. If you like, you eliminate fear by practise and this happens when you improve your skiing.

> *"The one who falls and gets up is so much stronger than the one who never fell."*
> **A Horoit**

I have skied with dozens of people over the years who just freeze when fear kicks in and feel they can no longer continue - unfortunately this is when accidents do happen. This is when you have to draw back on your experience whatever it is and try and get your rhythm and flow moving.

I came close to having 100 days on skis during the season and I skied at over a dozen different ski fields in France, Italy and Switzerland. When I arrived I felt like a fish out of water as I could not handle the steep and often way too difficult terrain. At times I felt like giving up on the off piste and just sticking to the piste skiing as I could not handle the real extreme skiing that attracted me in the first place.

I would often feel out of my depth and comfort zone. It really was like learning to ski all over again but it was also a lot to do with how hard I was prepared to push myself. I never gave up, got very fit and kept up with ski technology by changing skis to suit the variety of skiing I was doing. The result is that now I want more, I want another season. I want steeper and narrower, I want to ski faster. I want endless powder days that continue through your dreams until you get up and do it all over again. My urge for skiing has never been greater after all these years I simply want more.

It felt awesome, awe inspiring and amazing or what I call triple A skiing. Even after all these years, the deeper the snow the deeper my love grew!

"Powder snow skiing is not fun. It's life, fully lived, life lived in a blaze of reality."
Dolores La Chapelle, France

Changing skis to suit the terrain made a massive difference to my season. It is totally unrealistic for you to go out and buy a ski to suit every condition but every ski really does have its place and there is no bad ski. If you want to make short fast turns all day you need to be skiing on piste with a specialist slalom ski, they are super fast and turn quickly and accurately. If you want to extend those turns to a much wider and longer turn you should be on a giant slalom ski, once you learn the right technique you can ski as fast as you like on these skis but knowing you are in total control. If you want a bit of both slalom and giant slalom skiing on piste you need an all mountain terrain ski. When it comes to off piste skiing you can break down many skis to what percentage of use they suit both off piste and on. I tried a variety of these skis but then succumbed to the 100% fat off piste ski. The feeling underfoot is completely smooth and almost weightless and they turn very easily. There is a whole range of free rider skis with the twin tips that are great for tricks and the like. As Mark Gear suggested you have to change your technique a little but it is a complete new sensation and highly addictive. Skiing through fresh powder snow on fat skis is superlative and superior to any feeling I have had skiing. By the end of the season I ultimately understood what all the fuss was about skiing Chamonix. It was off piste and it was on fat skis!

Après skiing is also such a major part of enjoying the whole alpine experience as it is the number one social activity following day on the mountain; telling a friend or like minded skier is as close as you can get to trying to re-experience the highs and lows of the day, rest your sore muscles or simply soak up the magic atmosphere and often meeting someone to ski with the next day.

Another way to reminisce or enjoy skiing even more is by watching ski movies or main stream films that have some amazing skiing in them. Ski movies capture your imagination with action, adventure, thrills, romance and classic ski escapism. I have seen hundreds of ski movies and there is rarely a bad one because they all have skiing in them. Some might just have one ski scene, the other might be set in a romantic ski resort like Cortina and others are nothing but adrenalin packed from start to finish. I had also seen many amazing ski films on Chamonix such as the documentary Steep which made coming here all the more exciting.

> ***"Ski movies now days are all about high speed, huge air, showmanship, style, explosiveness, you know, just taking it to the mountain."***
> **Chris Davenport, Aspen, STEEP**

Ten of my top ski films, which are in no particular order, but to me are all part of developing my alpine experience and reliving past adventures, romanticising or anticipating new ones to come are(A couple of them are actually snowboard films but does it really matter what's under your feet?):

1. **James Bond, On Her Majesty's Secret Service:** I will start with the best of Bond as I am a huge fan. This is probably the most talked about James Bond film ever due to the fact that there was a love story and that they used a novice Australian actor George Lasenby to play James Bond. That however has no impact on the breathtaking mountain scenery and some of the best skiing ever to be seen on film at the time. Set mainly in the Swiss Alps and you can visit the location via Interlaken in Switzerland. **James Bond, For Yours Eyes Only:** Beautifully filmed on location in Cortina in Italy is a very alpine movie. Cortina is where the 1954 Winter Olympics were held and is a magnificent setting for most of this iconic flic. There is a fantastic ski chase when James first leaps the Olympic size ski jump and is then pursued by baddies on motor cross bikes with spikes in their wheels. There is also a little ice skating and a biathlon with the sensational background of the Italian Alps. I almost forgot **James Bond, The World is Not Enough** was also filmed around Chamonix and has some excellent skiing and an excellent ski chase in it. They ski down the glacier at the top of the Grand Montets and throughout the Chamonix valley with great shots of the Alps too! **A View To A Kills'** opening features high speed snowboarding before it was largely popular.

2. **Aspen Extreme:** Two ski buddies from Detroit go to Aspen to become ski instructors. The film was made in 1993 but seems more like an eighties movie when you watch it now. There is plenty of humour and romance set in one of the world's most famous ski resorts. There is excellent skiing throughout with the extreme competition for the finale. Still worth a watch today and I doubt Aspen has changed that much either.

3. **Downhill Racer:** Made in 1969 Robert Redford stars as a cocky skier who joins the US ski team. There is plenty of terrific skiing and the filming is surprisingly good considering when it was made and captures the speed and rush of the competitive side of the sport. "How fast must a man go to get from where he's at?" Redford must have liked the skiing as he went on to buy his own ski-field.

4. **The Pink Panther:** Even though the first Pink Panther film is not a ski movie by any means the setting is in the Swiss Alps. I fell in love with the elegant surroundings and the up-scale hotels of the ski resort and there is also some stunning alpine cinematography which has remained with me to this day. The classic ski gear, fashion and comical look at the mountains put it out on a limb. David Niven has a hilarious chapter in his book The Moon's a Balloon about filming in the Alps where he suffered a very unique type of below the belt frost bite!

5. **The Blizzard of AAHHH'S.** Some say The Blizzard is the most influential American ski movie ever made (mainly filmed in Chamonix). Made in 1988 it is essentially an extreme skiing documentary featuring two of the world's best ever extreme skiers, Scott Schmidt and Glen Plake. At the time no one had ever skied the terrain they skied, let alone filmed it – it remains a cult film in most skiing circles.

6. **Warren Miller, Journey:** Warren Miller has been making ski movies since 1949 and Journey is his 54th film. I have seen two thirds of these films and still remember the first I saw was back in the seventies in a packed hall in Twizel just before the ski season started. They are all worth watching but I thought Journey would be the perfect introduction. Miller popularised downhill skiing to the world on a global scale. His films have played a major part in the rapid growth of skiing throughout the world. He has a lifetime of experience framing,

choreographing and filming skiers and boarders which confirms his place at the top of the game. In Journey he takes us to Portillo Chile, Heavenly California, Aspen Colorado, Copper Mountains, Points North Alaska, Chamonix, Chugach Ranch Alaska, Bella Coola British Columbia, Morocco Africa, Helena Montana, Valbrunta Italy, The Canyons Resort Utah and Girwood and Winterlake Alaska.

"It's not about the destination, it's about the journey."
Warren Miller

7. **First Descent:** Okay so this is a snowboarding film and I am a passionate skier but this film blew me away. The film follows five snowboarding icons, Shaun White, Hannah Teter, Terje Haakonsen, Shawn Farmer and Nick Perata. On this epic Alaskan journey they ride the most challenging and dangerous mountains on the planet. It features some of the best snowboarding ever caught on film which tracks the rebellious, inspiring and sometimes controversial evolution of snowboarding from an underground American movement to a fully fledged global phenomenon.

8. **Steep:** A documentary made in 2007 about the world's best extreme skiers it follows them skiing places where no one has skied before. The film follows Doug Coombs, Chris Davenport, Ingrid Backstrom, Shane McConkey, Andrew McLean and Seth Morrison. These skiers constantly try and top themselves by attempting the seemingly impossible. When interviewed they say that extreme skiing puts them totally in the moment and gives them an appreciation of life so acute it makes the sport worth pursuing at all costs – one of them died in an avalanche during filming. Shot in high definition in Wyoming, France, British Columbia, Iceland and Alaska the film is a visual spectacle with a superior soundtrack. It also questions the risk verses pleasure argument and leaves you thinking is it worth it?

9. **That's it, That's all.** In a similar vain to first descent "That's it, that's all" follows a bunch of the world's best snowboarders around the globe. The film's main star is Travis Rice but it also stars Mark Lanvik, Nicolas Muller, Jeremy Jones,

Terje Haakonsen (First Descent), John Jackson and Scotty Lago. The first 15 minutes of the film starts off in Wanaka and Mount Cook, New Zealand the latter of which as I've mentioned was home during my teens. The cinematography and music captures the real essence of the New Zealand alpine experience perfectly and for this alone I give them Five Stars (Brilliant). They continue their adventures in Canada, Alaska and throughout the States. The sound track is sublime and these guys are at the top of their game, are just having a ball and it shows. There is a continuous flow of some of the best extreme snowboarding and especially jumping that you will ever see. The film must have cost a fortune to make as it has all the bells and whistles a big Hollywood blockbuster and probably the most helicopter shots I have seen in any film – unmissable!

> *"It's a chance to finally just shut your brain off and live within the moment".*
> **Travis Rice**

10. **Teton Gravity Research:** This film company makes some of the best extreme movies ever and makes Warren Miller films looks like Disney in comparison. TGR was started in 1995 by four extreme skiers who made the money to start the company from commercial fishing in Alaska. They have now made 18 feature films and a heap of extreme television programs. They also make snowboarding and surf movies and are at the cutting edge of action sports entertainment. They are continuously taking extreme skiing to a new level by trying what has never been done before. It's hard to say which my favourite is, as every time they make a new film that's it! I met one of their legendary skiers Kent Kreitler. The TGR produced movie "Reverence" is the story of his life. Kent had amazing energy, aura and presence - spiritual almost. God I would love to ski with him in the hope these qualities of his rubbed off on me. You here about these skiers that are really one with the mountains and Kent was a living example of this for me.

Top ten aside, Dick Barrymore, Roger Brown and Dick Darrence have also made some excellent ski movies. The opening scene of the James Bond film, The Spy Who Loved Me is outstanding and deserves a mention. The Heroes of Telemark has plenty of excellent cross country skiing in it and Hot Dog, Ski School and Better Off Dead, Dumb and Dumber deserve a special mention too and if you've not seen Walt Disney's The Art Of Skiing – a 1941 cartoon starring Goofy – you must, it's hilarious.

> ***"Anything that produces as much joy in peoples' lives is worth a certain amount of risk, physical risk, emotional risk, whatever, but how much risk is it worth is an open question."***
> **Lou Dawson, STEEP**

The subject of risk was an open question that was often discussed in Chamonix when someone you talked to was talking about their next extreme descent or off piste ski tour. It was also talked about especially after you heard about another death in the valley – everyone, of course, had an opinion.

My conclusion is that even though everyone does indeed have an opinion about what you do with your life it is totally up to you how much risk you take as long as you are not responsible for the death or injury of a less experienced skier. Skiing is very similar to its sister sport surfing as the world wide search for the highest wave is paralleled by the search for the steepest, wildest, most dangerous slopes and for perfect snow. This of course is all encouraged by what you read, what you see and what you hear about and also as technology advances so does confidence.

As more slopes are conquered you could also argue that what is left is un-skiable. Over the season the more I pushed myself obviously the higher the risk, but that risk comes with its own rewards, the more alive you feel and the greater the hunger for more. I now see the progression and the attraction to the extreme side and I want more of it. But I am not prepared to risk all like many of the extreme skiers I met. It all comes down to individual perceptions of what fear is, and what some skiers are prepared to do I am not. I do not want to die as I still have way too much to do in this life. And my conclusion by the end of the season is that there are way too many skiers taking way too many risks and the high death count is the result. If you want to play with fire eventually you will get burnt!

"I considered danger a kind of addiction, positive addiction. It's brain chemistry. It could be worse. It could be heroin. What's so bad about wanting to hold your own destiny in your own hands, even if just for a few seconds."
Wayne Sheldrake

Chamonix also hosted a series of different international ski events which included the FIS Slalom which was held at night time on a slope surrounded by forest and was excellent fun to watch. The Telemark International attracts the very best from around the world as does the Derby des Posettes - a cross country race but in teams of two. The free-ride world tour attracts the best in the world and was shown on large screens in the middle of town. The Junior World Championships were held in Chamonix when I was there as were the French Nationals. But my favourite event of the year was the annual Boss de Bosses.

The Boss Des Bosses is Europe's biggest inter-resort competition. Teams competed from Zermatt, Chamonix, Val d'Isere, Meribel, Courcheval and Verbier. Each team had to have seven male skiers, two female skiers, two telemark skiers and two snowboarders. The conditions in Chamonix were perfect for the 21st annual contest. The standard of skiing was unbelievable as the teams made their way down through massive moguls with a jump to complete just before the finish line. Heaps of fun and the party continued for a few nights and days in Chamonix with many still wearing their fancy dress outfits. In New Zealand the annual sevens competition is a sell-out 35,000 dress-up party and the Boss Des Bosses reminded me of it but on snow.

The skiing in Chamonix is without a doubt some of the very best in the world but wherever you are skiing is the ultimate place to be. If you are on skis with an uncontrollable smile, that's where the unsurpassed skiing is! There's just more if it in Chamonix!

"If there's no risk there's no adventure. I think adventure is a great part of life. For me it's why I am living, you know, it's to have some adventure."
Bill Briggs, legendary US extreme skier

Chapter Six
Chamonix Mountaineering

"Climb if you will but remember that courage and strength are nought without prudence, and that a momentary negligence may destroy the happiness of a lifetime. Do nothing in haste; look well to each step; and from the beginning think what might be the end."
Edward Whymper

Mountaineering is what first put Chamonix on the international map over 200 years ago and first cemented its fame and reputation today. It's what separates Chamonix Mont Blanc from other ski resorts and gives the area its much deserved standing as the birthplace of alpinism.

Having spent my high school years living in the footsteps of the New Zealand highest mountain range I had the opportunity to participate in plenty of climbing, hiking and tramping but had never ventured into rock or ice climbing as it I was honestly afraid I would seriously hurt myself.

My father was a keen tramper and climber until he had a family of four boys. In his teens he was a Queen's Scout and was chosen from thousands to represent New Zealand at the world Scout Jamboree in Austria in 1949. My parents also met on a tramping club ski trip and as dad was a great story teller he would fill us up with his alpine adventures and photographs.

My first experience of being in the mountains was during New Year's week in 1973 when we were back from Fiji visiting family and friends. We were staying with our cousins at an outdoor education centre at the top of the Southern Alps. We were very spoilt for scenic beauty in Fiji but I had never experienced anything like being in the mountains and that first experience laid a foundation for all my future alpine experiences - as it will for anyone when they first venture into any high altitude mountainous or alpine area.

When we shifted from the Solomon Islands, which is on the equator, to Twizel at 458 metres, or 1502 feet, at the foot of the Southern Alps and surrounded by stunning lakes. My two older brothers and I were as keen as mustard to go and climb a mountain. So dad took us to the local mountain shop where we bought tramping boots and suitable gear for the climb and off we went. We started at 800 metres at the base of Mount Cook which at 3754 metres, 12,316 feet, is the highest mountain in Australasia and then climbed for two hours to Searly Tans which is half way up to the famous Mueller Hut (it was officially re-opened in 2003 by Sir Edmund Hillary).

It was an unforgettable experience, the sensational views of New Zealand's highest snow clad peaks in your face, the crystalline beauty of the mountains, steep ice cliffs, monumental glaciers, vertical rock faces, glistening mountain lakes, long bushy snow tussock grass, the Edelweiss like Mount Cook Lilly, scree fields that were tremendous fun to run down, the thundering crash announcing the fall of a distance avalanche or the rending of a mighty glacier, you could also see and hear ice falling in the not so far distance as it made a bellowing and echoing sound throughout the Alps. From that moment I was hooked on all things alpine and have been to this day.

"Mountains are the beginning and end of all natural scenery"
John Ruskin

In my last year of high school I joined three teachers and a friend and we climbed that exact same slope to the Mueller Hut at the beginning of winter. We were planning a ski tour and decent. It's a 1000 metre vertical climb to the hut, peaking at 1800 metres and usually takes four hours. It had recently snowed and the forecast was for calm weather. We were climbing in our ski boots and gear using our poles for balance. Three quarters of the way up we were caught in a rapidly descending snow storm. My teachers were experienced mountaineers and even though I was very fit at the time I became completely exhausted, to the extent that my teachers had to carry my skis, pack and quite often me to the top.

It was snowing intemperately and there were monumental wind gusts. All I wanted to do was give-up and sleep – hypothermia would of course easily have killed me. I ate a good deal of Macintosh toffee, chocolate and a box of malted barley sugar to give me enough energy to continue. The snowstorm soon turned into a blizzard reaching sub zero temperatures creating almost white-out visibility. The only difference between a snowstorm and a blizzard is the strength of the wind and as the snow hits your face it stung like stinging nettle. The snow got deeper and deeper and almost impossible to climb through. My life was in the hands of my teachers who later admitted they had gone off the track a little. About four hours past our schedule and in the dark we eventually made it to the hut as the blizzard continued to torment us.

The Mueller hut was full of other keen skiers who were surprised to see us arrive so late. Like us, they were all dying to have their first ski run of the season as it was still weeks until the commercial ski fields opened. Looking back I have never been as exhausted or as close to death as I was on that climb. It instilled in me a lasting respect and fear of the mountains that I have to this day.

"We cannot command nature except by obeying her."
Francis Bacon

When we awoke the next morning it was magical as the storm had cleared and the Mueller Hut provides a 360 degree panorama of the surrounding Alps. There was two feet of fresh snow which proved perfect to ski in as the temperature was still well below zero. As we skied down we witnessed avalanches and large amounts of ice fall - the noise like thunder in a tropical rain storm. I felt as alive and as happy as I ever had.

Being brought up in the Southern Alps meant we were taught all aspects of alpinism through the school's outdoor education centre but I never got hooked to the extent where I went out and bought climbing gear. My near death experience at age 17 was enough to put me off ever putting myself in that sort of helpless position again. But I have always been fascinated with climbers that risk all to find that happiness which is so complete for them.

Sir Edmund Hillary has been a mentor and inspiration for thousands of New Zealand climbers and Kiwis are renowned for being some of the best mountaineers and guides found anywhere in the world. I was lucky enough to catch up with one of them, who now lives in Chamonix, Russell

Brice. I also became very interested in Sir Edmund's achievements and his climbing of Everest for the first time when I read the screenplay written by good friend Tom Scott. Tom has also produced, written and presented a series of documentaries about Sir Edmund's life in the Himalayas that are well worth a watch. Like Chamonix, New Zealand has its own Alpine Museum at the base of Mount Cook which is dedicated to the great man.

"You climb for the hell of it."
Sir Edmund Hillary

Once you've spent time in Chamonix it is impossible not to be inspired by the landscape. The mountains were the biggest I had ever seen and there are spires, peaks, glaciers and ice falls everywhere you look - when you see it for the first time it blows your mind. It is a timeless land full of adventure and hope and it is easy to see the attraction for climbers.

To fully appreciate the valley, and as importantly to paint the fullest picture of its origins, would be impossible without delving into mountaineering history as Chamonix is where it all started. During my quest to meet as many people as possible for the book I met hundreds of experienced and passionate climbers.

The first I met was a 40 something Irish climber Sean Murphy, who in April 2009 like many others went for a beer at the Bar Les Sports in hope of finding a guide with whom to climb Mont Blanc sometime during his stay. After a long afternoon enjoying a Guinness or two Sean finally met a guide who insisted that if they left immediately they could catch the last telecabin up the Aguille du Midi as the conditions were perfect.

So away they went, full of Guinness, running furiously to catch the last lift. They then rested at the Cosmiques refuge with a ton of other enthusiastic climbers and started the assent at 10pm making it to the top at dawn. What an incredible way to see sunrise if not perhaps a little overcrowded. I heard hundreds of similar stories throughout the season and although the climb is not meant to be technically overly difficult well over 1000 people have died trying – so the statistics say it has the highest fatality rate of any mountain by far. By comparison, more than 500 have died attempting the Matterhorn, 200 on Everest, 100 on K2 and some 70 on the north face of the Eiger.

> **"Boundaries are only formed by a limitation of one's imagination."**
> **Tim Emmett**

Climbing is as important to the local economy in Chamonix as skiing and has brought the town as much fame especially as climbing is popular all year round. Its rich and varied history sets Chamonix apart compared to other resorts proving that there is far more to the alpine experience than just skiing. Personally you might not like the idea of climbing due to the dangerous nature of the sport but the history and famous escapades undertaken in this valley should be retold and respected by all.

Chamonix first became famous internationally in 1741 when two young English aristocrats, William Windham and Richard Pocock, discovered the valley. They arrived accompanied by men at arms and guards and were unsure of the welcome they would receive especially as there is a well documented history of war and tension between the two countries.

Surprisingly their reception was a warm one and they are deeply impressed by the valley and surrounding summits. They ventured up the mountain in direction of the Mer de Glace (Sea of ice) It is the subsequent recital of their visit to this small mountain village and the glaciers that has an impact on the whole of Europe. As a result wealthy tourists, in particular the English come to admire the mysterious Mer de Glace.

Artists, writers, scientists and soldiers were drawn to the foot of Mont Blanc, a visit which becomes an essential part of their European tour. The first inn in Chamonix opened in 1770 and marked the early development of the hotel trade and the first mountaineering exploits. The conquest of Mont Blanc in 1786 by Dr Michel Paccard and Jacques Balamat contributes to the demystification of the summits and seals the destiny of the Chamonix mountain community. The first luxury hotel was built in 1816 and the hotel industry continued to grow throughout the 1800s, crowned by three splendid palaces built in the early 1900's.

> **"A man does not climb a mountain without bringing some of it away with him, and leaving something of himself upon it."**
> **Sir Martin Conway**

Certain dates are synonymous with the development of summer tourism: the creation of the Compagnie des Guides de Chamonix in 1821 and the inauguration of the Montenvers-Mer du Glace cog railway in 1908. There are many famous climbing families in Chamonix whose status is legendary not only in France but throughout the climbing world. There is a series of published books in red hardback covers filled with brilliant stories and photographs of their escapades, adventures, first summits, heroics such as famous rescues and of course deaths. Unfortunately the series is only in French and very much an expensive collectors' item.

The 1860s and 1870s was the golden age of Victorian climbing and thus climbing became popular throughout Europe. However initially climbing was very elite as it was a very expensive sport and only accessible to the really rich such as Edward Whymper - the first man to climb the Matterhorn. He was also the first to climb the Aiguille Vert above the Grand Montets ski field.

His first accent of the Matterhorn took place on July 14th 1865. Only Whymper, then 25, and two Zermatt guides, the Taugwalders, father and son came back from the adventure alive. The rope they climbed with was incredibly thin and had broken which resulted in the death of four others. The rope is on display in the Zermatt museum.

Edward Whymper is buried in the Chamonix graveyard and almost all serious climbers for some reason pay a visit to his grave so I decided to as well. His grave is the second you see on the left as you enter and his headstone is shaped like the Matterhorn itself. I can recommend his book Scrambles in the Alps as an engrossing read.

In 1853 Albert Smith a well known British satirist and entrepreneur staged a show about his accent of Mont Blanc in 1851 in the Egyptian hall in Piccadilly. The show had a six year sell out run and in the summer of 1855, according to the times, Britain was gripped with Mont Blanc mania. The show inspired tens of thousands of people to see Mont Blanc.

> *"The fact that people were killed now and again was inspiring for those who weren't, because it kept the possibility of death at least in sight, and that was essential to the mountain experience".*
> **Robert MacFarlane, Mountains of the Mind**

The most famous of all climbing adventures of the time was achieved by the French and by two men who were both guides in Chamonix, Maurice Herzog and Louis Lachenal. In 1950, they were the first two climbers to climb one of the worlds fourteen 8,000 metre peaks, Annapurna. Maurice

Herzog wrote a book about the adventure selling over ten million copies making it the best selling climbing book of all time. As a result of losing his gloves he suffered terrible frost bite losing most his fingers and both he and Lachenal lost all of their toes. The consequent gangrene required the expedition doctor to perform emergency amputations in the field without anaesthetic.

I visited both the Argentiere and Chamonix graveyards and found them to be filled with hundreds of climbers who, as far as I am concerned, all died way too young but they died doing what they loved most as Anne Sauvy's quote perfectly summarises at the end of this chapter.

I am not much of a graveyard enthusiast but if anything was to signify and clarify the enormity of death in this area this was it. If you are not a local you are given a temporary spot in the graveyard which after a couple of years has to be moved. I heard of many stories where the French threatened to dig up bodies if they were not collected - only in France.

The climbers I talked to all see death as a reality they could be faced with at any time very much like the extreme skiers who come to Chamonix. Every year on August 14th and 15th all the local guides have two days to remember the guides they have lost that year and to remember other guides who died in the line of duty. The event is called the Fete du Guides (Mountain Guides' Festival). The festival offers an innovative mixture of creativity corresponding to the ambitions of young guides along with an ardent respect for the guides' long standing tradition.

The first day combines a sound and light show, created and performed on the rock face by the guides themselves as well as a firework display and concert. The next day is the traditional ceremony. All the guides are present, in costume, with ropes and ice axes -similar to how Australians and New Zealanders celebrate and commemorate ANZAC Day. There is a large procession in the morning to Chamonix's cemetery in remembrance of guides and alpinists lost to the mountains and a wreath of flowers is placed in the cemetery and a role call for the entire list of guides is called out. The Compagnie's president evokes the chosen theme of the festival, which each year associates history with tradition and current affairs. Then there is the awarding of medals to the newly initiated guides by their mentors; awarding of medals of merit for difficulty and consistency to well deserved clients. Then there is the blessing of ropes and ice-axes before the great mass of August 15th. Stands and aperitifs follow at midday to officially close the ceremony.

The Compagnie des Guides has lost four guides a year on average since they were first formed in 1821. The reason they were formed in the first place was because of the death of two guides in 1820. The Compagnie was formed to ensure the families of the guides were protected financially. To become a member of this prestigious and very traditional guiding company you have to be born in the area but there are a few exceptions such as mountain guide Jean Pierre Devouassoux who was a Monchu - a foreigner to Chamonix - not a Chamoniarde, a local.

He was an exception to the rule but he proved his exceptional guiding, climbing and mountaineering skills time and again. His status is now legendary and many books have been written about him. Did you know that in France that if you are in a position where you can help someone in danger and you chose not to it is a criminal offence?

There is a book which I found inspirational, sobering and fascinating. Mountain Rescue-Chamonix Mont Blanc by French author Anne Sauvy who has written nine popular books, is a keen climber and made over 170 alpine ascents and has also won a bunch of literary awards.

The book was only translated into English by her publisher a few years ago. Anne spent three months with the mountain rescue service in the summer season of 1997. I doubt whether much has changed since then apart from an increase in rescues as the popularity of alpinism increases. Mountain going has been one of the fastest growing leisure activities in the past 25 years. Global sales of outdoor products and services are now well over ten billion pounds.

The mountain rescue service is based in Chamonix and covers rescues throughout the valley and all the massifs. It has become a highly skilled and speedy operation that lifts stricken climbers from huge glaciers, the famed local rock peaks and the hazardous snow slopes. It is run by a section of the Gendarmerie the PGHM. The gendarmes are skilled mountaineers and they in turn support mountaineer doctors who are often need to conduct urgent medical tasks in dangerous situations.

In her book every aspect of the rescues are observed such as strange incidents, the big technical rescues, the modest alarms looking for lost children or ageing relatives, high altitude ailments, eccentric soloists in trouble, parapent plummets, potential epics averted and sad terminal mishaps. In my research for this book I bought and read anything I could find on Chamonix and this book is on the top of my list as it is beautifully written with dignity and respect for both the rescuers themselves and alpinism itself.

> **"Everyone wants to live at the top of the mountain but all the happiness occurs while you are climbing it".**
> **Confucius**

Chamonix also hosts the Mountain Climbing World Cup - three days during which the world's best climbers from all over the globe challenge each other at the heart of the world capital of alpinism. The event has been running successfully for ten years in Chamonix and continues to grow in numbers which is indicative of climbing's popularity. The standard also gets harder every year as climbers push their limits further and further.

The glaciers in Chamonix are almost as celebrated as the mountains so I paid a visit to the glacier museum to find out more. There are seven major glaciers and several smaller ones in the valley. The largest is the Mer de Glace (Sea of Ice). It is the second largest glacier in the European Alps and moves at 90 cm and recedes seven and a half metres per year.

Around 1700 during a period of severe winters the Mer de Glace threatened to obstruct the Arve valley so the local inhabitants resorted to exorcism of the evil glacier spirits in hope of halting the great wall of ice. Incidentally the largest glacier in the Alps is the Aletsch Glacier in Switzerland. Climbers, skiers, hikers, artist, writers, poets and tourists have been drawn to their beauty and character since the valley was first discovered.

> **"The warnings about global warming have been extremely clear for a long time. We are facing a global climate crisis. It is deepening. We are entering a period of consequences."**
> **Al Gore**

Glaciers form through repeated freezing and thawing of snow layers. Settled snow undergoes structural changes, which increase its density. This compaction results in a completely bonded zone of rigid ice. This layer is subject to fracturing and cracking forming crevasses as the glacial mass slowly moves down hill. Immense internal pressure raises the ice's melting point and the resultant melt-water acts as a lubricant. Most glacial movement is due to the ice's own plasticity. Ice crystals deformed by the huge weight above, slide over each other, much as discs of shiny plastic would.

Glaciers are dangerous, risky and totally unpredictable as they are always moving and if you gave the above to a skier to read before they were about to ski a glacier many would have second thoughts. However, when you ski over them, through them or underneath them you are transposed into another world of unsurpassed beauty whilst climbers enjoy the variety that they offer.

The Chamonix and Mont Blanc also has a long history of crystal collecting and are very famous for the fine alpine minerals which I witnessed firsthand at the Chamonix Crystal museum. Many of the collectors were tough, rugged mountaineers who made their fortunes collecting Quartz, Amethyst and Pink Fluorite.

As I have mentioned earlier Russell Brice the legendary New Zealand mountain climber and guide set up a successful business in Chamonix many years ago. Russell is a world renowned climbing legend and I was especially excited to catch up with him. Neil Heil the author who wrote the book Dark Summit described Russell as intimidating with the air of a seasoned General who had built a successful career out of an extraordinary game and that high altitude guiding came with its own set of rules and complications.

I got to have Russell around for dinner and cook for him as Kikki, manager of the Gite le Belvédère, was a good friend of his French journalist wife Caroline. Caroline was real hoot, a tall buxom blonde, attractive and very outgoing unlike Russell who has a much quieter and more reserved demeanour. She and I hit it off and chatted often when Russell took off to the Himalayas she would pop around to see Kikki.

She made it very easy to talk to Russell. Patrick a young Irishman staying at the Gite joined in as well as he often did. I think my being from New Zealand certainly helped and Russell clearly enjoyed Patrick's youthful energy and humour. Russell did not have children of his own due to the lifestyle he had chosen but he had a great rapport with Patrick. I was appreciative he was there as I would imagine it would be hard normally to get Russell to open up as I was sure that he was initially not that interested in talking about his illustrious career with the likes of me.

The reason I thought it important to talk with him was to confirm the significance of Climbing to the overall alpine experience in Chamonix. Russell has been a household name in international climbing circles for over 20 years. He owns three companies. The Chamonix Experience, The Mountain Experience, which specialises in taking people climbing in the Himalayas, and Himex which is his high mountain experience company.

I first heard of him many years ago when he climbed the 30 highest peaks in New Zealand all in one climbing season. Although some have tried no one has repeated this achievement. Russell was also very close friends with Sir Edmund Hillary who treated him like a son and he was by his side when Sir Edmund lost his wife Louise and daughter Belinda to a horrific plane crash in Kathmandu in 1975. There are comparisons between the two men and having such a mentor has had a major impact on the continuing success of Russell's mountaineering and guiding career. Both have climbed Everest, both have spent their careers donating time, money and effort to helping the Sherpas and both are very modest, humble and honest human beings.

Russell's guiding company in the Himalayas has guided over 500 people to Everest base camp and he holds a record for the most summits without ever losing a client. In the Himalayas he is a household name and he is called Big Boss by the Sherpas. He has played a key role in over 15 mountain rescues on Everest. In 1998 along with fellow climber Harry Taylor he was the first to cross the Pinnacles on Everest, an infamous trio of spires high above the north-east ridge that looks like a cluster of shark's teeth. The discovery channel chose Russell and his company to film the hit reality BBC television series Beyond the Limit.

Well you can imagine how excited I was to be having dinner with him. Luckily Russell obviously enjoyed mine and Patrick's company to the extent that he bid his wife and Kikki goodnight and stayed up with us until the early hours of the morning and all the Burgundy and a whole bottle of Scotch had gone – the fact that I had once done the same with Sir Edmund I hope impressed Russell

> **"It's not their job (Sherpas) to die alongside you because of your ambitions."**
> **Russell Brice**

Russell has been climbing in Chamonix for over 30 years and initially like other guides would go prospecting to the local bar to find his clients. He has now made it to the top of Mont Blanc close to 100 times and his company has taken thousands of clients to the summit. Like any stranger trying to start a business in Chamonix, but especially in the most traditional of them all, it took umpteen years for the local guides to accept him. His impeccable and unquestionable record spoke for itself.

During the evening he entrusted me with lots of stories that were off the record but others that weren't, such as the time he was shot when mistaken for a Tibet refugee.

The next day when Patrick and I were way too hung-over to ski but tried very hard to determine what I could and couldn't write about. Patrick also discovered that he had Russell's car keys - he had given him to take two beautiful girls back to Verbier that day and his last words the previous evening were: "Good luck with the girls Patrick".

"Climb high, climb far. Your goal the sky, your aim the stars."
School moto

Russell's business in Chamonix had grown steadily through word of mouth and he catered to an almost 100% English speaking clientele. He is reputed to having the best and toughest guides found anywhere in the world working for him in both Chamonix and the Himalayas. After many years he has hired a vast number of experienced international guides and when possible he hires New Zealanders as he finds them to be the very best in the business.

One reason being that in New Zealand when you go climbing, you have to walk for miles and miles before you even get to the bottom of the mountain. By contrast if you take Mont Blanc as an example, you can take a telecabin to 3,800 meters and all you have to do is climb another 1000. In New Zealand this is perceived as a joke in mountain climbing circles.

Back to the more serious part of my conversation with Russell because climbing is without question one of the most dangerous sports in the world and many say Russell's success is due to his impeccable organisational skills. I was honestly surprised that he had never succumbed to the many offers he has had by publishers and authors to having a book written about him. His answer to me was that a lot of things beyond one's control happen on the mountain and that is where they should stay. For him climbing is personal to him and those with him and is no one else's business. Russell by his own admission has lost over 80% of his friends to climbing, so I could easily see his point.

"I see my path, but I don't know where it leads. Not knowing where I'm going is what inspires me."
Rosalia de Castro

I talked to another renowned English mountaineer, guide and skier Kenton Cool whose guiding business is based in Chamonix. My initial reaction to meeting Kenton was that he would be the ideal person to play Sir Edmund Hillary when the film of his life gets made. Kenton's image could easily be portrayed as the James Bond of mountain climbing, suave, handsome, confident and gifted with a sense of occasion - he has already climbed Everest eight times and twice in one week in 2007. His Facebook photo has him wearing black tie and holding an ice axe over his shoulder and is about as Bond as you can get.

Most recently he skied down from the summit of Mount Manaslu which is over 8.000 metres. He previously successfully climbed the north face of the Eiger and then Everest guiding 65 year old Sir Ralph Fiennes (who was once seriously considered for the role of James Bond), helping raise over two million pounds for charity.

Kenton and his business partner Guy Willet run Dream Guides in Chamonix which offers almost everything imaginable in the pursuit of adventure from mountain expeditions to the world's highest peaks, ice climbing, ski touring and ski expeditions to alpine climbing the likes of Mont Blanc and off piste and back country skiing. At only 37 years old Kenton is a climber that is set to break all sorts of records and someone whose adventures are worth following

There are also some very entertaining and thrilling climbing movies and even though hard nose climbers dispute the reality, some of the photography should be commended. These films glorify courage and draw on the essence of their adventures. Thousands of people have started climbing as a result of watching one or two of them and many will have you on the edge of your seat at some stage – or possibly give you vertigo. Ten that are definitely worth a watch:

1. **The Eiger Sanction.** This 1975 movie was directed by and stars Clint Eastwood who doubles as a University Professor, avid art collector and part time professional killer. He is forced out of retirement to take one last job by joining a climb of the Eiger to eliminate one of the climbers. There is some brilliant climbing cinematography in both Switzerland and in Zion national park and is a must see for climbing fans.

> *"Tell me, Mr Bowman, in your opinion do these men climb to prove their manhood, or is it more a matter of compensating for inferiority feelings."*
> **Female journalist**

2. **Everest.** Everest is a 44 minute documentary that is narrated by Liam Neeson. It was shown in Imax theatres for many years and follows a group of climbers making their ascent in spring 1996. The sweeping Imax cinematography is breathtaking, the vistas of the Himalayas are nothing short of spectacular. Some of the camera angles have to be seen to be believed. During filming a huge blizzard hit the mountain and nearly two dozen people were trapped and five died. Amongst them was Rob Hall a very well known and experienced New Zealand climber and good friend of Russell Brice. His last phone call to his wife rips your guts out.

3. **The North Face.** Based on a true story it's a suspense filled adventure about a competition to climb the most dangerous rock face in the Alps. Set in 1936, as Nazi propaganda urges the nation's alpinists to conquer the unclimbed north face of the Swiss Massif- the Eiger. What is great is that there is no obvious use of computer generated images, it's authentically German and the use of old equipment, sets, and scenes gives you a very realistic feel for alpinism of the day.

4. **K2.** This 1991 movie tells the story of two climbing friends that join a team bound for the world's second highest peak K2 which is also renowned as the hardest mountain in the world to climb. The film is very eighties and you can see where they got the idea for Vertical Limit from as there are distinct similarities. While the acting and plot can be criticised the reason you watch a film like this in the first place is in hope of seeing some excellent climbing and if you watch it with that goal, you will not be disappointed.

5. **Touching the Void.** This is a documentary about two climbers who climbed to the summit of Mount Siul Grande in Peru in 1985. This feat had been previously attempted but never achieved. They reach the peak but on the descent one of the climbers falls and breaks his ankle and as he is being lowered he slips and falls 300 meters, leaving both climbers dangling. In

order to survive the other has no choice but to cut the rope. The climber falls a great distance breaking his leg. He is seriously hurt and left for dead but somehow he miraculously survives and crawls out to freedom over a period of seven days. This is an extraordinary story of survival against the odds told with humour and realism. It is also thought provoking – should he really have cut the rope? Brilliant!

6. **Cliff Hanger.** This 1993 Sylvester Stallone action flick is reminiscent of a Die Hard film but set in the Rockies. Okay this is a very main stream Hollywood film about one man against the odds but the climbing scenes right from the very beginning are fantastic. Stallone could easily be a mountain guide and he had the best in the business to help make the climbing scenes as realistic as possible. Fast forward to the good bits.

7. **Where Eagles Dare:** Although not a climbing movie as such there are some excellent climbing scenes in this Alistair McLean thriller that will have you on the edge of your seat. It is stunningly filmed in the Bavarian Alps and set during world war two when an American General is held prisoner in a mountain top castle.

8. **Premier de Cordee 1945.** Adapted from a famous Roger Frison-Roche novel. the film is of course set in the Chamonix valley and is based around a father and son relationship. The son wants to become a guide while his father wants him to become a hotelier. The movie was actually made in 1943 during German occupation. The photography is outstanding and especially seeing the valley back then. I have only watched it in French without subtitles just to witness the cinematography and even so, it is well worth a watch.

9. **Vertical Limit.** This big budget American flick is bit of a joke and has many flaws such as taking plutonium above eight thousand metres. The story rotates around a brother and a team of climbers being paid big bucks to rescue his sister and a billionaire who are trapped near the top of K2. The opening scene is stolen from Cliff Hanger but worth seeing and there are some great climbing shots and cinematography which of course is filmed in New Zealand.

10. **Off The Edge.** This is a 1976 New Zealand documentary that was nominated for an Oscar. The film covers a couple of climbers

who climb to a hut high up in the New Zealand Southern Alps before skiing and hang gliding their way down through the mountains. This has always been a personal favourite of mine as it was shot very close to my home in Twizel!

The opening scene of Mission Impossible deserves a special mention as does the climbing in the finale of James Bond, For Your Eyes Only. Did you know that James Bond author Ian Fleming lost both his parents in a climbing accident in Chamonix?

> *"I was making a film called The White Tower at the foot of Mont Blanc – the one thing I learned from that experience was that's it more difficult to go down a mountain than go up."*
> **Glen Ford**

For the life of me though, I still do not understand why there has not been a film made about the greatest achievement in climbing ever, the conquest of Mount Everest in 1953 by none other than Sir Edmund Hillary.

Okay so potentially I am a little biased but I promise you if this achievement was done by an American, Asian, Englishman or European you would probably be watching the third or fourth version of the film on screen. Certainly filming any movie with a great amount of climbing is a very expensive endeavour and thus why such a film has not been made to date.

Few people in the world have seen as many movies as I have and I promise you the life of Sir Edmund would make an astonishing film if it captured the essence of his true character. Think Shackleton, Scott, Amundsen, Whymper all of whom have had their great adventures turned into film. Sir Edmund was a phenomenal human being as his whole life was about giving and contributing and wanting nothing back in return.

His life was also a tragic as he lost the love of his life and his daughter as they came to join him in the Himalayas while he was continuing his charity work for the Sherpas. Work that no government could do and work that he continued until the day he died. How he ended up being the chosen one to climb Everest is as close to fate as I will ever believe in and is a brilliant story.

When a state funeral was held in New Zealand it broadcast live on national television and the whole country came to a halt to pay tribute and show respect to Sir Edmund as there has never been such a humble and well respected New Zealander. His life and how he risked all to make it to the summit of Everest along with Sherpa Tensing Noring would make a glorious piece of cinema. I rest my case!

Spending the winter season in Chamonix has totally convinced me I want to come back and spend more time in these iconic mountains and to climb to the summit of Mont Blanc. I have grown a deep respect for the Chamonix guides who risk much in pursuit of what they love and most of all I have totally fallen in love with highest French Alps of them all which have seduced me, inspired me and impelled me thus far to a higher ground.

> *"Those who choose effort, cold, burning sunshine, remoteness, bracing air, distant horizons, snow studded with sequins, the sunbeam of a serac seemingly giving birth to an emerald, the serrated ice, the light and the azure – if they die for their passion, they died not for nothing, however tragic and distressing their death may be. For they are part of those through mankind keeps its grandeur."*
> **Anne Sauvy, Mountain Rescue Chamonix Mont Blanc**

Chapter Seven
Chamonix's hospitality

*"Be courteous to all, but intimate with few; and let those be
well tried before you give them your confidence."*
George Washington

Before I arrived in Chamonix I had heard many mostly positive reports
about the world famous après skiing and hospitality which has always been
promoted as equally matching the spectacular skiing. Almost as much as
hitting the slopes I was looking forward to finding my way round the local
social scene of restaurants, hotels and bars and discovering what they had
to offer. As mentioned I have owned, or co-owned a number of restaurants,
bars and nightclubs over what is nearly 20 years. I am still very passionate
about the business and love trying and finding spots that I really like. I
am also a very social creature and love a good party atmosphere full of
like minded people.

Few international resorts can boast such a rich and colourful history
as to what went on behind the scenes when the sun went down. Spending
a whole season in Chamonix you can choose to go to bars and restaurants
that suit all budgets, styles and tastes.

Chamonix was once full of luxurious five star hotels and the rich
and famous from all over the world came to marvel at Mont Blanc to
experience the Alps at their most luxurious. It was an extravagant time
but also an exciting one as there were still many peaks in the valley which
remained unconquered. Lord Byron and Mary Shellie, who of course wrote
Frankenstein in 1818, were regular visitors to the area and much of their
inspiration was sought here.

Some of the famous luxury hotels were The Chamonix Place Hotel, The Hotel du Paris, The Grand Hotel, The Majestic, The Savoy Palace and the Hotel d'Angleterre but sadly most of them have now been turned into apartment blocks or the likes of Club Med. There are photos of all these hotels in the Alpine Museum in Chamonix. These hotels clearly indicated that the alpine experience was not accessible to everyone.

The rich used to gather in these hotels and watch from the balconies as the climbers attempting first accents. Often the attraction was the expectation of death, which was often the case, a spectator sport which could be compared to slaves fighting to their deaths as gladiators in the arena while the wealthy spectators marvelled enjoying their champagne.

Until recently for some years there were no longer any Five Star rated Hotels in France which is ridiculous as there are many such at the luxurious Hotel Du Cap in Antibes on the French Riviera. The Carlton Intercontinental in Cannes was awarded the first fifth star in 2010. The fifth star is a result of a change in French law which lead to a change in the hotel rating system. To qualify a hotel has to comply with 300 different standards relating to the quality of service, equipment, comfort, disabled access, environmental issues and new technologies. I mention this as Chamonix now has the potential to lure the tourist who only ever stays in a Five Star establishment.

Will Chamonix ever see those bygone days again, such as in the 1960s when you could walk into the famous Hotel de Paris and witness Bridget Bardot sipping champagne with alpinist Lionel Terray. Alpinists were more like movie stars and celebrities back then and those images can still be seen in Chamonix today. The luxurious foundations Chamonix was built on has instilled a sense of heritage, culture and spirit of adventure that continues throughout the valley, and often late into the night.

Chamonix has continued to bloom throughout the years and was chosen as the most suitable resort to hold the first Olympics in 1924. Hosting the event came with benefits that continue to enhance the valley's fame today but also initiated a visual theme and established the town's iconic brand that has stuck to this day.

Many of the hotels, chalets, bars and restaurants continue to use distinctive images of the past - the Art Deco classics such as a 1920s poster of a couple taking a ski jump can still be seen all over town. These art nouvelle images continue to be used throughout other resorts and have done much to strengthen the European ski resort brand and image.

Chamonix is still an expensive town, but show me and internationally acclaimed ski resort that isn't. It comes down to simple economics of supply and demand. This is not necessarily a good thing as it breeds complacency and arrogance - something you could argue is all part of the French hospitality experience. Such a home court advantage is somewhat reflected in the hospitality for tourists but for seasoniares, it is a case of familiarity breeds contempt.

So let me start at the top of the scale in what I experienced of its hospitality and I will work my way down. I must admit there are a few bars I did not bother to visit but hopefully my explorations will give you a real feel for Chamonix night-life.

For the more discerning there are up-market hotels such as the four star Albert the 1st or the four star modern Morgane Hotel. These hotels all have upmarket swanky cocktail bars often attracting the rich and famous. If it's your ambition to hang out in a comfortable ski resort hotel bar and not venture into the unknown so be it. No matter where you go out in Chamonix there is no concrete sense of style or a particularly obvious fashion, it's very eclectic and influenced by its proximity to Italy and Switzerland - perhaps this has something to do with the fact that it's a town where 10,000 people live and not just a purpose-built resort. There is no overt outrageous luxury or accordingly overly exorbitant prices which you will find in nearby Verbier or Megeve.

What is interesting, and I have seen at first hand, is that there is no doubt that Chamonix still attracts the rich and famous, but it is not flaunted around and it is not that apparent. Perhaps that is why the resort appeals to the likes of Tiger Woods or some of the world's wealthiest industrialists one of whom was staying in a Hip Chalet.

Being in Chamonix for the season you witness the rhythm of the town, when it's busy and when it's not. Some nights you can go out and every bar, restaurant and club is full to the brim, the town is alive and the atmosphere magical – at other times it feels like a ghost town. Chamonix, more than any other resort in Europe attracts a higher percentage of men than any other ski resort. The statistics quoted on the street are 82% men and you will often walk into a bar thinking there is a gay convention on in town. However it is not always the case and plenty of bars are full of beautiful woman. I met hundreds of wonderful woman throughout the season and luckily some are even still talking to me and I'm in contact with them to this day.

> *"Now is the time to get drunk - on wine, poetry, or on virtue,*
> *as you please."*
> **Charles Baudelaire**

After skiing most people feel like they have popped a Viagra, even women you would usually consider unattractive look like Marilyn Monroe. It's a simple and proven recipe I can assure you; mountain air, adrenalin and your physical atonement will mean you are either tired and exhausted from a lack of fitness or that your body is on fire and subconsciously your want more, but the lifts are closed and the obvious next best thing is sex. So let's face it, if sex is what you are after in a ski resort and you are having difficulty I recommend professional help.

And to this end there is something for all ages, including venues like The Mix Bar. Often referred to by the locals as the Cougar Bar - the reason being a reputation for older wealthier woman as its core clientele, preying on fresh young blood in the form of young skiers or snowboarders who can't afford to buy a drink: it seems to work and is certainly the cheapest form of prostitution I have ever seen. These sort of bars maintain a legendary status throughout the Alps and books have been written and movies made - you know the story, a couple of ski bums with no money head to the Alps, meet rich divorcee, heiress or the like and live the life of Riley in a mutually satisfying relationship. (The movie Aspen Extreme. Comes to mind.)

If you are not willing to sell your soul there are plenty of dirty, scummy but fun underground type bars in Chamonix for the younger budget conscious or just plain broke ski bum. These bars are distinctive as you can smell the body odour of unwashed skiers and boarders leaking out onto the street like steam from a hot Jacuzzi in the snow. These bars are mainly popularised by first year or hard core seasonaires and for the average visitor don't warrant a mention, but their popularity confirms their place. I doubt the financial longevity of these types of establishments but I am happy to be proven wrong.

There are also English styled bars, pubs and restaurants throughout the valley which cater to the British, Australian and regrettably New Zealand market. One thing I see repeatedly, but fail to comprehend, is that when people travel they often just want to go to a bar or restaurant that is completely the same as the one around the corner from where they live.

To me these travellers are missing out on an authentic and local experience that is right at their doorstep.

I saw this a good deal when I was cooking for guests and a lot of the time they hired a private chef so they could be guaranteed food they were familiar with. Having been a regular international traveller for the past 25 years I hate the trends in much planetary hospitality such as leaving home and never even meeting someone who speaks the local language. It happens in Chamonix all the time, from the time you are picked up at the airport to meeting your English ski instructor and having your restaurant bookings taken care of. There is even an English gentleman's styled club, aptly named The Clubhouse. It's upmarket and well furnished but as it was I did not come all the way to Chamonix to drink tea and enjoy Sunday roast with flush English men and woman while exchanging inane pleasantries.

> *"If you reject the food, ignore the customs, fear the religion and avoid the people, you might better off stay at home."*
> **James Michener**

As a New Zealander looking in, the relationship between France and the United Kingdom is a bizarre one. In Chamonix which is 55% occupied by Brits in the winter season, you seldom see the two socialising together. Without a doubt their relationship is a co-dependent one but that was not always so. They have a very extensive history and its interesting seeing it from another point of view.

It was also the English who first climbed the majority of the French peaks which must piss them off no end! Many of the English I talked to think many French are obnoxious, lazy, stuck-up and rude while the French think the British are ignorant as they do not make the effort to integrate, but the French are certainly happy to have them as tourists or residents. All in all it's a bit of fun how they get on but you do have to commend the British for their sense of adventure and the fact that they were responsible for the initial growth of both skiing and alpine tourism.

> *"The urge to explore the earth and subdue it, which has made England the great colonizer of the world, and led individual Englishmen to the wildest recesses of every continent."*
> **Robert Macfarlane, Mountains of the Mind**

Let's face it, you either want a holiday to relax and unwind, to learn or to seek adventure in a life that probably lacks it mostly. Rather than integrating, enjoy and appreciate France for what it is and the potentially authentic lifestyle that is clearly available the English would rather set up bits of 'home' but with better weather, bigger houses, or for the adventure offered by the Alps.

What is clear to me, having visited both countries is that France offers stunningly beautiful alpine country with an ever changing climate and landscape that the UK is very lucky to have on its door step. While Britain is green and lush there are few spots, other than some of its historic ones like Durham, the Lake District and the Scottish Highlands that are worth venturing to for an outdoors holiday and let's be honest, the weather sucks. As much as France needs Sterling and as much as the United Kingdom needs France it's a shame that the relationship between the two is not of a friendlier nature.

France was also recently voted to have the best life style in the world for the fifth time in a row. The scoring categories are cost of living, environment, leisure and culture, economy, freedom, health, infrastructure, safety and climate. The other four places in order were: Australia, Switzerland, Germany and New Zealand - the United Kingdom was placed 25th.

When you dig beneath the surface of Chamonix's hospitality you will discover excellent bars and restaurants that are often 100% French. They are often not found on the tourist radar but discovered by word of mouth recommendations. They will welcome you with open arms as opposed to some of the visitor spots that are often so sick of bloody tourists that their food and poor service reflects just that.

The thing you either love or hate about the French is that they do everything in their own time and if service is slow or pedantic the more stressed you get about it the more glee it gives them and the slower they move; it's the inverse proportion rule. Do not judge a restaurant or bar by expensive glossy advertisings in swanky magazines but ask around, it gives you the opportunity of meeting a few new people as well. I love French hospitality no matter what form it comes in. They are masters at the trade even though a little arrogant.

Chamonix is also not overpopulated by bars and restaurants so you are usually guaranteed a comfortable atmosphere unless it is very, very quiet in town anyway. During peak times everything will be full so plan your holiday in advance and do the same with your restaurant bookings. The recession has had an effect on skiing especially corporate weekends, there was a time when during peak season every bar and restaurant in Chamonix was completely full but now there are only a couple that don't offer a happy hour to attract punters. It will make a monumental difference to your stay in Chamonix if you enjoy the French way of doing things.

There is without question a dark underbelly that comes hand in hand with any international ski resort. There is an obvious and often witnessed drug culture as mountains and extreme highs seem to perfectly complement each other. You know it's all about getting high in whatever form it comes in as many skiers just want the rush to continue.

There is also gambling as Chamonix has a Casino lit up like a Christmas tree in the middle of town. Chamonix also offers table dancing, stripping, a gay bar, infidelity and prostitution thrown into the night-life mix which was a little hard to find out about in the local tourist guides. However I do not believe there are any swingers' bars in Chamonix but I could be wrong!

The spicy scene is not that conspicuous but it is there for you if you can't live without it. There is no denying that for some the allure of the mountains is to drink, socialise, party hard, drink some more and maybe even throw some skiing into the mix.

Having been to other famous ski resorts like St Moritz, St Anton, Val d'Isere and Verbier I would have to conclude that Chamonix lacks a defining romantic feel - probably as it is overshadowed by the dominance of men. I'm a romantic and fall in love at the drop of a snowflake but didn't come to Chamonix looking for it. Over the entire season after meeting at least 2000 people - which includes the hundreds of five to ten minute conversations on ski lifts and the like - I met only three couples who found each other in Chamonix.

George (Dynamic Lives) met his English wife in a bar; Dave from The Office met Gabriella at the Vagabond and Pistol Pete and Cecile met skiing at La Tour. Sure there are plenty of women that come to Chamonix but generalising I would have to say the majority of them are hard core mountain types most of whom are in peak fitness many of them surpassing the men in both mountaineering and ski/board skills.

Chamonix can't be all things to all people, you can't maintain this extreme last frontier image if you want to also attract the romantic at heart. Anything alpine is romantic for sure, the breathtaking scenery, glaciers, snow falling, log fires, naked in the Jacuzzi drinking Crystal etc. but in Chamonix it is overshadowed by rugged, macho and alpinism - that's the way they want to keep it and that's just the way it is folks.

The standard of food in Chamonix overall is pretty damn good especially if you like big hearty meals which reflects its provincial heritage and alpine cuisine. Many of the restaurants offer the traditional local food which is all based on peasant food – it's not spectacular but it is very edible and enjoyable and I will talk about it in greater detail a little later in the book.

There are also some outstanding restaurants in Chamonix such as dining at the legendary Albert Premier which has two Michelin Stars. The Carrier family that own it and the adjoining restaurant The Mason de Carrier are one of the oldest established families in Chamonix and have been running Albert 1st for five generations. It was first mentioned in the Michelin guide way back in 1925.

Last year they released their own cookbook titled Stars & Mont Blanc which took over a year to make as it covers the four seasons of their cuisine and of mountain living. Throughout the book they have a variety of special guests joining them for a drink in the Quartz bar or for lunch or dinner. The book gives you a wondrous feel for their family's history in the valley, their astounding culinary art and of the fascinating people that helped mould Chamonix into the legendary status of today. The recipes are of the spectacular cuisine they serve throughout the year. The gastronomy photography by Philippe Schaff and high altitude photography by Anthony Lamiche alone is worth buying the book for. For the cover shot of the book a group of them climbed to the top of Mont Blanc and set up a table for two with white linen, fine china, crystal glasses and silverware.

The Mason de Carrier restaurant atmosphere comes from the farmhouse setting of a bygone era with antiques, art and photos throughout the restaurant showing the history of the town. Like many of the other restaurants they have their own gardens supplying as much fresh produce as possible. The Albert 1st is a blend of Le Corbusier's contemporary furnishings with antiques and art depicting the area.

I was lucky enough to meet a few members of the family and take a tour of their 20,000 bottle wine cellar – it was one of the highlights of my whole stay. The Carrier family have produced guides, alpinists and many have skied for France over the years. They are an institution and if you have a passion for food and wine one of their restaurants or their equally up-market bar, the Quartz Bar, is a must visit. The Carriers and Pierre Maillet set the benchmark for all things culinary in Chamonix.

I must also mention the contemporary chic Morgane hotel in the centre of Chamonix as the one Michelin star Le Bistrot is also a must visit for all the culinary cognoscenti. But I am not here to provide a dining guide and if I was I have just mentioned three of the very best you will find anywhere in the Chamonix valley that have passed the test of time.

If there is a good restaurant in town that you really want to find out about you will by tapping into the fantastic word of mouth network. Just ask someone on the chairlift, your ski instructor or in a bar as a good recommendation is the best advice you will get. It's how I found out about Le Bergerie at Brevant ski field.

My personal favourite of the season was the 15 Euro three course special at La Dahu Hotel in Argentiere as the food was provincially French, authentic and excellent value.

The bars I spent the most time at all had the best and friendliest service as well as the liveliest atmospheres. There was the MBC bar just on the outskirts of Chamonix which was owned by four Canadians who brewed their own micro beer, it was always busy and great fun and often had live music. The service was always prompt and exceptionally friendly and a very easy place to talk to anyone.

There was the Vagabond where I spent New Year's Eve which always had excellent music or a DJ and a trendy vibe to follow. Its bar is very small, full of old stone and wood with an open log fire and offers the best selection of single malts in Chamonix as the owner is an enthusiastic collector. I never had a bad night there and the English style pub food was wholesome and good value. They also boast some of the best and friendliest service in the valley.

Then there was Chamber Neuf, the infamous Swedish bar, where après skiing started early afternoon but really kicked-in when the live music started and which soon filled every table with people dancing, many still with their ski boots on. Anthems like U2's Where the Streets have No Name or Sweet Home Alabama could be heard at the other end of Chamonix and I am sure has caused a few avalanches in its day.

In Chamonix Sud there was the other Swedish legend, the South Bar which was comparable to being in down town Stockholm as it was usually full to the brim with Swedes. It was a cool bar although the crowd a little young for my tastes - but for Scandie eye candy a must see.

The other coolish bar of note in Chamonix is Le Vert which is Australian/English owned and managed and a couple of kilometres out towards Les Houches. Le Vert also has accommodation and room to move with a comfortable lounge type atmosphere and DJs playing the latest hip tunes. Later in the season they were responsible for Sunday afternoon sounds at the top of the Planpraz - sunshine, deck chairs to lounge in whilst admiring Mont Blanc and the surrounding Alps. Perfect!

Back up in Argentiere there were five superb bars/restaurants that I spent time in. There was the Savoy, which had the best après ski atmosphere in the small village, and was like a much smaller version of Chamber Neuf (and also Swedish owned). I also loved Le Rencard which was French owned and operated and home to the mono-board Museum – there are re mono-boards hung on all the walls creating a very lively eighties vibe. It was impossible to go there without having a shot or two of Genepi or Chartreuse and always the first round was shouted by the management.

There was also the Le Rusticana - I thought the interior design was a little too contemporary to fit the historic alpine village atmosphere - but they served superior food and wine, were wonderful hosts and always busy. The owner was British and years ago was one of only 27 people that worked for Microsoft United Kingdom but he came to Chamonix, fell in love with the place and never left.

I also spent time at the French owned and operated Slalom bar. It was tiny, on a corner with a cosy outdoor balcony and usually packed full of local French people but always with a lively atmosphere and a special cocktail of the day. There were also many places I tried which were great fun such as the Irish bar The Jeckle and the Mexican restaurant and bar The Cantina.

Looking back over the entire season I spent most of my time at a bar called The Office. Everyone who goes loved being called there on their mobiles: "I'm at the office". You can get the picture. My initial attraction was the stunning Swedish blonde Emelie who worked behind the bar and I even wrote her a poem as I would often sit there after skiing and write notes for this book. Emelie was a competitive figure skater in her youth and I have always had a thing for ice skaters and skiers

Here is the poem I wrote which I have had to recall from my initial notes as I gave the other copy it to Emelie as soon as I had written it.

SWEDEN- Maypole, Abba, Ekland, Nobel, Saab, Volvo, Zorn, Garbo,
The Bergman's Ingmar and Ingrid, Absolut and Emelie
Your guess is as good as mine what brought her here to Chamonix.
She has a smile impossible to forget
Awakening, refreshing and sincere when we met.
Gifted with presence and occasion to every customer in the Office bar
Personality, flair, the stunning looks of a star.

It's impossible for me to sit at this table and not to write
When there is such grace, finesse and panache in sight.
Such words Emelie should hear every day
Shouted from the top of the Grand Montets.
I am sure most people would definitely agree with my written word
So forgive me Emelie if a stranger writing is bordering absurd.
But I like to tell people what I think
And pen to paper, my communication link.
Wouldn't the world be a better place
If daily, you could put a smile on another face.
Aspiration and inspiration brought me to the French Alps so high
Your honest cheerfulness and vitality is something money can't buy.
I am here to finish my novel and screenplay
And meeting you inspires me to write all day.

The Australian owner Dave Elliot is probably the optimum host in the Chamonix valley. Big, outgoing, friendly, charming and exuberant; he was very popular with locals and visitors alike and spoke fluent French and Italian but maintained a bear-down Aussie accent.

Everybody it seemed knew him and when I was first looking for accommodation people would often say to me, have you asked Dave? The first night I met him was at the opening party of Evolution Two, a ski school in Chamonix. It was held at his opposition's bar and restaurant, Le Rusticana, but Dave came along brining his own bottle of red wine and I thought he was our host until I was formally introduced.

What I also like about Dave is that he greeted everyone - well men that is - with a handshake and he was more than happy to kiss all the female clientele. Dave was also a very generous host and there would never be a night when he was not buying someone a shot and took great glee in watching the impact of his home made concoctions. He sure loved every minute of his job.

His alpine story was that he tried snowboarding once but it was in 1996 when he went to Whistler for three weeks at the age of 24 that he absolutely fell in love with it. In 2000 he went to Verbier - which he did not enjoy, especially the 75 Euros per night fee for the hostel.

It was there though that he met people who raved about Chamonix (as they would) so he moved to the valley. He stayed at the Vagabond and on his first night he met the love of his life, Gabrielle who is Italian. There are thousands of international travellers like Dave who turn up at a ski resort, fall in love with the place and never leave and I met hundreds of people with similar stories.

What I also loved about the Office Bar is that most nights there was some form of entertainment. Friday and Saturday they had an excellent DJ, Monday a popular band and Wednesday the locals would have a talent night where anyone who could sing or play a musical instrument was welcome to join in. I also loved the fact that everyone brought their dogs with them and often there were up to ten of them having a whale of a time as their owners got drunk. Hark, hark the dogs do bark, the beggars are coming to town was very much the Office atmosphere.

I also met a ton of people there who have helped me with this book. During the 2010 Winter Olympics I almost moved in. There was indeed something magical about watching my first Winter Olympics in the snow, as close as I can imagine to being there that's for sure.

Every single night you hit the town in a international ski resort such as Chamonix is a new adventure as the weather patterns change such and bring the excitement and celebration of new snow; the peak of the season when there are way more people than usual around; the quieter but often much more alcoholic infused nights with chalet staff and a few other seasonaires; the nights out after a superb powder day where everyone was on fire and dying to share their stories and the level of energy is like being at a rock concert. There were also many nights dining at fine restaurants and continuing on with a night cap or ten; there were the big nights, massive nights out in Chamonix where you would visit at least a dozen bars but have to hitch-hike or walk the 8km back to Argentiere as there was no public transport at 3am. Most memorable was the occasion when I was offered a large quantity of cash by an elderly French gentleman in exchange for selling him Patrick for the night. I said sure, but funnily enough Patrick wasn't game!

One thing I can definitely say about Chamonix is that the public transport sucks - and the taxis cost a fortune. The last bus back to Argentiere is at midnight, just when the night-life is warming up in town. There is a train that runs from Saint Gervais to Vallorcine but it only runs every hour and stops at 9.00pm. The buses are periodic and although they connect you to all the ski fields they are seldom reliable especially around lunch time – I guess the drivers are probably arguing about whose lunch break it is.

Remember also a big advantage of coming to Chamonix is that you can enjoy the best of Italian and Swiss hospitality as well. There are countless first-class restaurants, traditional pizzerias, tratatorias, stylish bars and cafés in Courmayeur. And if you want a bit of premium Swiss hospitality, nearby Verbier is full to the brim with world class restaurants and bars.

Chamonix's hospitality status is certainly as much a part of the alpine experience as all other facets that are offered here. There is something for everyone and I am sure all the establishments I have mentioned will be around for many a year to come.

"As long as I retain my feeling and passion for nature, I can partly soften or subdue other passions and resist or endure those of others.
Lord Byron

Chapter Eight
Food, wine and cooking Alpine style.

"The mountains bring together the past, the present and the future in the same way that culinary art tells of where we come from, who we are and where we are heading. Every time Antonio and I come to Mont Blanc, I feel the entrancing charm of this environment; a sensation of eternity. The mountains invite discovery of the power of nature."
Nadia Santini; Stars & Mont Blanc

Over the season as my skiing progressed I became preoccupied with information gathering for the book you have been reading and this of course leads me on to food and wine. This chapter's objective is to instil in you what I learnt mainly about the local cuisine but also European alpine food and cooking in general during ski season. What you will like about this chapter is just how easy cooking Haute-Savoie food is.

As mentioned I have been a partner in or owner of a number of successful restaurants and have always been a passionate cook - I was confident in the kitchen since I can't remember when. At high school I argued the merits of joining the girls' cooking class so convincingly that my teachers gave in and let me join the home economics class. A first in New Zealand but many more followed suit. I took the class instead of the boys only metal and woodwork classes which I found monotonous, and also difficult, whereas cooking I found a breeze.

At school we used to organise progressive dinners where we would have different courses at about four or five different houses. In my last year at school I worked at a ski lodge where I would often help the chef cook. I have thrown dinner parties since I can remember and have been in and out of event management during my career which has included organising four large wine and food festivals culminating in the Marlborough Wine and Food Festival which attracted more than 9000 guests, 55 wineries and 30 restaurants.

In my travels my thoughts are, first and foremost, consumed with all things culinary and coming to Chamonix was no different and the food and wine was going to be as much a part of my alpine experience as anything else. Food reflects ones culture and heritage more than anything else for me and I was looking forward to learning.

Initially I felt a little out of my depth but I took life in the luxury chalet market like a duck to water. Before I arrived in Chamonix I had spent hours and hours Googling and printing out all sorts of alpine recipes in preparation for my trip. I emailed many chef friends back in New Zealand who had cooked in France for recipe ideas etc. I also read as many books on Haute-Savoie cuisine as possible.

My brother Peter is a very good cook and his wife Vikki makes the foremost salads I have ever tasted. They have a large collection of cook books which I read from back to front when I stayed with them in Zurich. I did make a few mistakes along the way, like my schoolboy error in not covering up some lamb shanks that I was slow roasting in the oven for five hours and that emerged as dry as a Driza-Bone.

> *"If more of us valued food and cheer and song above hoarded gold, it would be a merrier world."*
> **J.R.R Tolkien**

By the end of the season I certainly feel I mastered the local way of cooking as well as having an in-depth knowledge of Haute-Savoie cuisine. Cooking in this style is honestly not that hard and I had many guests complementing me on my food as some of the best they had ever tried in the Alps. Confidence, passion and the willingness to give anything a go are paramount in the kitchen for me.

It is also incredible what you remember from previously cooking a dish as your taste buds have an extraordinary memory. The scene in the movie Ratatouille when the food critic tries the dish and suddenly it brings back a kaleidoscope of memories is perfectly true. I have planned hundreds of menus for restaurants as well as spending countless hours with my chefs discussing new menus and recipes. I have also spent a great deal of time watching my chefs prepare food and this combined with watching videos of experts chefs cook, is all fodder for the mind that can be repeated when you cook yourself. The only difference I believe between a great chef and a good one is passion, time and education.

"My cooking is a question of passion, of experience, mechanics, intuition, confidence, flair, imagination & creativity and least of all recipes."
Anon

In the Alps I was finding a huge contentment and satisfaction in learning alpine cuisine. I love how you think when you cook and how the mind goes through a series of thought patterns. The day's skiing finished and satisfied, classical music on the stereo, a glass of your favourite red in a tall round crystal glass, a flash in a pan with aromas filling the house with an awesome smell, and someone special to cook for is a perfect way to spend time, any-time.

"There is no love sincerer than the love of food."
George Bernard Shaw (1856-1950)

There is something deeply enriching for the soul that can only be found in cooking for others and people that do not cook or are not passionate about food are missing one of the most pleasurable gifts this world has to offer. I am certain of this. All of the luxury chalets I cooked in Chamonix bar one, had open kitchens so I could talk to the guests as the aroma aroused their taste buds.

As skiing is a very physical, tiring sport and you build up a large appetite and the perfect dish is a good hearty meal. Over the entire season as my extreme skiing progressed, in a similar way so did my cooking.

The Executive Chef job presented me with the opportunity to cook almost what I liked as long as the client agreed to the menus I had prepared for them. I was particularly interested in cooking and learning more about alpine food and not necessarily just from France. As mentioned I had skied in Austria, Switzerland and Italy and wanted to try my hand at their styles of alpine cooking especially as most of the necessary ingredients were readily available. First and foremost though, I went to great lengths to introduce myself to and learn all aspects that I could of Haute-Savoie cuisine. It was the local fare after all and the recipes were all reasonably simple providing you used the correct localised produce and stuck to recipe and cooking time guide lines.

I have had the opportunity of visiting most of the famous food producing regions of France and this experience helped me understand where Haute-Savoie cuisine fits in to the bigger picture. France is the second largest agricultural producer in the world beaten only by the USA. You could easily spend your life learning about French cuisine as many have done. Its diversity is legendary; the south of France is famous for its Mediterranean influences with dishes such as Nicoise and Bouillabaisse; the Dordogne notable for duck, black truffles, Foie Gras and walnuts; Brittany famous for crepes and mussels; Alsace with its strongly Germanic influences, Burgundy famed for Beouf Bourguignon or Coq au Vin; the Pyrenees with its Spanish influences such as chilli, Serrano and Bayonne ham; the Languedoc for Cassoulet and Roquefort; Bordeaux celebrated for duck confit; the Atlantic coast for oysters; Normandy most notable for Brie and Camembert; Paris for being eclectic and Lyon for being the richest food region in the country. In order to fully respect and appreciate it you must also understand the significance of baking and patisserie as they are part of everyday life. I mention these regions to help explain the significance of Haute-Savoie and how over the winter I moved from knowing very little to being something of a professional.

I found out that Haute-Savoie is equally as important a region for French cuisine as any other and has had influences on more modern day France. The Haute-Savoie area only became part of France in 1860 and the traditional local fare reflects the rugged lives of alpine farmers. Their diet consisted of plenty of cheese, cured bacon and potatoes. The cooking of Haute-Savoie, like that of most mountain food, is more sturdy than artful. Waverley Root called the cooking of alpine France coarse, unsubtle and stern. In his book **The Food of France** (Alfred A. Knopf), he wondered whether the diet of mountain people contributes to "their sometimes truculent independence." Still, the Savoie menu, with its gratins of cabbages and root vegetables stewed in milk or broth, cornmeal pies stuffed with shredded birds, crude flat breads topped with cheese and fruit, fondues and giant stews, is indisputably French and fundamentally good and very uncomplicated to cook.

"When a man's stomach is full it makes no difference whether he is rich or poor."
Euripides (BC 480-BC 406)

The first thing you will probably hear about food in Chamonix is the Tartiflette – perhaps the most gratifying dish in all of France's Haute-Savoie and without doubt the region's speciality. Sure, every restaurant in Chamonix will more than likely serve a Tartiflette and some are just plain awful – it's an easy dish to cook but like anything over or under cooked and its ruined - but is all part of the dining alpine experience and a must try.

The dish has the serrated wrack and satisfaction of macaroni and cheese baked until it forms a chewy crust, the pure pleasure derived from a bowl of creamy baked potatoes and a flavour that could only come from 500 years spent perfecting cheese-making. A clump of cream-soaked potato and a smoky bit of lardon will be married with a smooth coat of Reblochon cheese made from the milk of one of three breeds of French cows that march to the alpine meadows in the spring and return to hay-filled barns in the winter.

The trick is the Reblochon, which is sliced over the top before the dish is baked. It's a soft, washed-rind round cheese about as thick as a paperback copy of Lord of the Rings. A good one has savour and aroma and a slightly salty quality. The bad are as bland and rubbery as cheap Brie.

At its best when the cows are eating nothing but alpine grass, the cheese got its name from 16th-century farmers who were sick of the tax on their milk. They'd milk their cows until they were about halfway done, pay the tax on that bounty and then finish the job. They had to do something with the remaining milk to avoid charges of tax evasion. So they made cheese, the name of which comes from the word reblocher, which means to milk again. (Some tie the name to the slang term "reblessa," which in the local dialect basically means to steal.)

To make Tartiflette the whole cheese is sliced in half horizontally and turned cut side down before the dish goes in the oven. The idea is to turn the soft, brushed rind into a crispy crust as the inside of the cheese melts into the cream and coats the potatoes.

For an alpine-weary traveller looking for a regional dish, Tartiflette is inexpensive and accessible. You can't argue with the instant comfort that comes from a bubbling hot dish of cheese, bacon and potatoes and it really is the perfect dish to have after skiing. The health conscious could argue that the dish will solidify in your stomach for many days as it's very hard to digest, but hey do you want the full alpine experience or not?

Another popular dish is Raclette - where you melt the cheese under your own table top grill on top of a potato whilst a hot plate on top cooks your bacon and vegetables. It livens up any restaurant with burnt cheesy smells and the sizzling of the hot plate and it's great fun and easy way to eat especially if you are with a group of friends – so too is sharing a Pierade, a hot stone which is used as a grilling plate at your table. You can smell these flavours leaking out onto the street enticing people in when you walk through the centre of Chamonix in the evening.

I soon found out that pork is one of the pillars of Savoie cuisine. It is also very reasonably priced and, along with chicken, the cheapest meat that you can buy locally. Really cheap.

Traditionally Pork was used a lot because it was easy to use and preserve - an important consideration when snowed in for the winter. Along with cows I did not see a single pig in the Chamonix valley, but they are definitely around somewhere judging by the amount of pork you see being consumed.

As well as being essential ingredients in many Savoyard dishes, pork offal, bacon, streaky bacon, cheeks and fillets form the basis of a wide range of hams and sausages. The locals have long used two techniques to conserve meat: salting and smoking, with smoking being known from Gallo-Roman times. The area's numerous specialities include several types of sausage, such as Diots, Pormoniers de Tarentaise, Pormonaises de Haute-Savoie, Longeôles and Saucisses de Magland, together with saucissons made from donkey and goat meat, and mutton ham from Valloire.

> **"One cannot think well, love well, sleep well, if one has not dined well."**
> **Virginia Woolf**

I found that different types of hams are also common fodder in the valley and quite different to both the Spanish and Italian varieties which I was more used to before my stay. The meat used for making hams is rigorously selected and is salted with soft salt for two to three weeks (depending on the size the joint), and then kiln-seasoned and left to rest at ambient temperature for a few days, allowing it to naturally achieve a nice pink colour. It is matured by hanging in a sort of ventilated attic in natural air for a period five to six months. During this long stage, a layer of lard is applied to the cut ends to prevent any loss of moisture and to let the ham's natural flavours develop. The result is this fine delicate beautifully textured ham that has a variety of flavours depending on your tastes. The hams were also great for lunch on the mountain with a fresh baguette and cheese. It is quite interesting to see.

Jambom cru is a very traditional ham similar to Parma ham which is preserved with saltpetre, salt and sugar that was readily available. I always wanted to buy the whole leg like we do at Christmas time in New Zealand!

I loved using sausages for lunches on the mountain as they can be eaten easily at any time. I liked making up large Anti pastas after skiing where I used a lot of different sausages and cured meats.

My favourite sausages during the season were Diots which are lightly-textured and tender sausages - one of Savoie's great traditional dishes. They can be made entirely from pork or from a mixture of pork and beef. Top quality ingredients (wild boar, goat, donkey, pork) are also used for making saucisson (a large dry filled sausage). Coarsely chopped meat is taken as a sign of quality, as it prevents too much fat being added. The resulting mixture is seasoned and then stuffed into natural skins. The saucissons are then kiln-seasoned and dried and are marvellous.

"Good food ends with good talk."
Geoffrey Neighor

But of all Haute-Savoie's local products, cheeses are without a doubt at the very top of their cuisine as all their dishes are almost all centred around it I spent the season eating way too much cheese but luckily I skied most of it off – but I still have a bit of a cheese belly that needs a little work!

The region is a first-rate cheese-making area with a large number of cooperative (fruitière) and farmhouse producers. The area has no fewer than five AOC cheeses: Reblochon, Beaufort, Tome des Bauges, Abondance and Chevrotin. In addition, Emmental and Tomme de Savoie are governed by an IGP guaranteeing their provenance and production conditions.

"Cheese is milk's leap toward immortality."
Clifton Fadiman (1904-1999)

Like all cuisine eating is believing and I always find cooking reviews, recipes, cooking magazines etc. a little frustrating as you are light years away from the tasting sensation until you have tried it yourself. Anyway the history of these cheeses is well worth a read alone.

Other, less well-known cheeses are produced in smaller quantities, including Tamié, Bleu de Termignon, Persilé des Aravis, Sérac and Vacherin. The only thing I feel you need to know about serving cheese is take it out of the fridge at least three hours before serving so it reaches room temperature. I also like the French way of eating cheese by having it before desert not after. Cheese-making is very simple when you understand the fundamentals as is becoming a connoisseur, the more you eat the more you know.

The Savoie Mont Blanc's rivers are full of trout and its lakes are home to many species of fish, including members of the salmon family, such as Lavaret and arctic char, and coarse fish, such as pike or perch. This wide range has inspired a large number of original and inventive dishes that are superbly accompanied by a delicious local white wine. I cooked with fresh pike and perch by baking them with butter, garlic and tinfoil with herbs de Provence. In New Zealand it is forbidden to fish trout or river salmon commercially or eat them in a restaurant. There is something very alpine about catching your fish in a high altitude mountain lake and then cooking it along with other regional produce. Many escaped prisoners in World War Two enjoyed these species of fish while trying to make it over the French Alps to the Swiss Boarder.

> *"A woman should never be seen eating or drinking, unless it be lobster salad and Champagne, the only true feminine and becoming viands."*
> **Lord Byron (1788-1824)**

Haute-Savoie, I can happily say produces a very good range of different wines, they may not be the very best wines that France produce, but they certainly match the food of the area. But is there anything better when visiting a region for the very first time than trying their wines and matching them with the local produce?

Savoie's vineyards produce a surprising variety of wines, covering four AOCs (appellation d'origine contrôlee), 22 vintages and 23 grape varieties. With this diversity comes a multiplicity of flavours and bouquets that will delight even the most demanding palette if only for a glass. The wines are lighter in style than those I am used to and it took me a little while to fully appreciate them. The wines all have very distinctive labels ensuring you will easily recognise that they are from the Haute-Savoie.

The wine-growing areas of Savoie Mont Blanc are the Combe de Savoie, the banks of Lake Bourget, Chautagne, Seyssel, Frangy, the Arve Valley and the shores of Lake Geneva - these wines have been known since antiquity. White wines are made from **Jacquère**, **Altesse**, **Chasselas**, **Gringet** and **Roussanne** grapes; red wines from **Mondeuse**, **Gamay** and **Pinot**. Savoie's fruity and light-coloured white wines are best enjoyed chilled, as an aperitif or as an accompaniment for fish, seafood and hors d'oeuvres, for cheese, or, of course, for fondue or Tartiflette. I am told they are beautiful to visit in the summer or at harvest.

> *"I can see that you certainly know your wine. Most of the guests that stay here wouldn't know the difference between a Bordeaux and a claret."*
> **John Cleese (Basil Fawlty) Fawlty Towers 1975**

The region's **sparkling wines** (Ayze, Seyssel and Pétillant de Savoie) can also be savoured as aperitifs or with dessert. The **red and rosé wines** made from Gamay grapes are perfect with main courses, cooked meats and Savoie cheeses, whereas the richer, more ample Mondeuse provides an ideal complement for red meat and game dishes. These wines can be laid down for around five years but I think they are best drunk now. I matched the reds with lamb and venison and they were a pretty good match.

Any alpine experience in any of the European Alps would not nearly be complete without digestives after a long meal, especially considering the amount of cheese and butter in the local food. The most popular local digestive spirit is Genepi which has a floral type bouquet as is it is made with a high altitude mountain flower. It might take a little getting used, to due to its very high alcohol content, but is really is the perfect way to finish a meal or prepare oneself for a big night ahead. Eau de Vie (water of life) is another popular strong spirit commonly taken as a shot and it will knock your socks off as will green chartreuse. Cognacs and Armagnac are especially common for the French in Chamonix and I especially enjoy a glass or two after lunch, after dinner, after skiing or even during skiing on an especially cold day. Digestives are also a perfect compliment with hot chocolate especially Chartreuse.

> *"Worthless people love only to eat and drink; people of worth eat and drink only to live."*
> *Socrates (BC 469-BC 399)*

The area is of course famous for producing mineral water and you have to ask, often more than once, for tap water in Chamonix - which is ridiculous because most of the god damn water is at your footsteps. The qualities of the waters of **Evian-les-Bains**, **Thonon-les-Bains** and **Aix-les-Bains** are renowned throughout the world. Evian water is produced by rain and snow-melt water filtering through abed of glacial sand and the three peaks on the bottle are best seen when you are skiing Flegere as they are directly across from you. Thonon water takes its source on the Versoie Plateau, from where it trickles through sands and clays, absorbing minerals as it goes, before emerging at a temperature of 13°C. Its diuretic properties have been recognised since Roman times. Aix water is a light and lightly mineralised water containing bicarbonates of calcium and magnesium that is bottled at Grésy sur Aix.

The local beers have quickly gained a reputation for their character and for the fact that they are brewed using mineral water: **La Souveraine**, **La Cordée** is a pure-malt, craft-made beer fermented with bilberries rather than hops and is a little too fruity for me. **La Blanche du Mont Blanc** is a light lager made from malt, wheat, hops, coriander and orange and is surprisingly good. There is nothing liking drinking beer that you actually think is good for you, which is how they market it in Chamonix.

I cooked a variety local dishes over the season for guests and friends and always included some form of local produce whether it be an anti-pasta to start or a Tartiflette for the main course or cheese to finish. I cooked a Boulanger gratin with stock, butter, potatoes, onions topped with lamb or gratin Dauphinoise which is made with potatoes, butter, garlic, cream and nutmeg. I certainly wasn't convinced that the local food was all there was to a high altitude or ski week diet so I cooked dishes that were well known in the Swiss, Austrian and Italian Alps and compared notes on what influence it had in Haute-Savoie.

It is often ridiculous what the restaurants in Chamonix serve for lunch as it is way too high in fat and hard to digest. I have no problem cooking these dishes for dinner though. After lunch your energy would be consumed digesting these sort of cooked cheese, bacon, cream and potato dishes. I always carry a trail mix of nuts, chocolate and dried fruit which gives me energy continuously throughout the day. And water of course, as you dehydrate up the mountain very easily.

My brother Peter and his family have lived in Germany, Austria and now Switzerland and I have visited them regularly over the years and have always tried as much local food as possible. I was soon to find out that Alpine cuisine is very similar no matter where you go and it is usually a very hardy type meal. In Austria my favourite alpine dish is Tiroler Grostel - a stir fry mix of meat, potatoes, onions and herbs served in a heavy cast iron pan. You will find Weiner schnitzel in almost every ski resort in the world but the best is found in Switzerland, Germany and Austria. It is best served with a potato Rosti and unique local onion gravy, but many just like having it with chips.

The best sausages and beer combination comes from Germany where you are served sausages with sour kraut, chips and mustards and/or with gravy. The alpine cuisine in Switzerland is a diverse as the landscape as it borders on five different countries. I prefer the German speaking side as I love German sausages, sour kraut, schnitzels and especially the German beer. In Italy they take their food a little more seriously in the Alps, large anti-pastas, salads, cured meats, hot homemade pasta dishes and a variety of cooked meats. In the Alps you will find pasta, pizza, the local play on sandwiches, goulash, stews, etc.

I had a ball cooking all these cuisines. There was seldom a night when I was not cooking and every night I would try another wine or two while matching it with the food. It is true that many of the wines in France are cheaper than beer and often cheaper than Coca Cola. They are excellent value for money whilst, most importantly, still maintaining quality control. It is not true that you can only buy French wine in super markets, wine shops, restaurants, bars, hotels etc. but is often the case. If you do not want to drink French wine take a look around and you will find Italian or Spanish. In Metro the large cash and carry sold a good variety of international and new world wines for all palates and price points.

As this is a food chapter I must include my top ten food movies that are all a must see for anyone passionate about food and cooking. At the top of my list is the 1987 Danish film Babette's Feast, 2) Tampopo, 3) Eat Drink Man Woman, 4) Like Water for Chocolate, 5) Mostly Martha, 6) Dinner Rush, 7) Big Night, 8) Sideways, 9) Julie & Julia, 10) The Cook the Thief his Wife and her Lover or maybe Chocolat.

I would not say the winter season in Chamonix made me more passionate about cuisine as I have always remained faithful to my prying palate. However I relished every single new taste and cooking experience and this education and knowledge will remain with me forever and a day.

> *"He who loves not wine, woman and song remains a fool his whole life long."*
> **Johann Heinrich Voss 1777**

Chapter Nine
New friends and a Gite

"Old friends pass away, new friends appear. It is just like the days. An old day passes, a new day arrives. The important thing is to make it meaningful: a meaningful friend - or a meaningful day."
Dalai Lama

It was purely by chance that I ended up staying at the Gite le Belvédère (the Belvédère) with a roster of some 50 or so people for the rest of the ski season. I had been staying at a lovely little French hotel called Les Randoneurs for about three weeks and was really enjoying it. It had a wonderful little restaurant and a dinky wooden bar where I would often have a pint of the local tap beer while writing or talking to the other guests.

It too was also across the road from the Grand Montets ski field and had stunning views. It was the middle of February and as I finally had no bookings I went to visit my older brother Peter, his wife Vikki and daughters Antonia and Helena in Zurich. Peter is a high school teacher, and manages the Zurich International School ski team. I enjoyed a few days skiing with him when they race trained at Elm not far from the city. Elm is home to Vreni Schneider who I met while skiing there. She was voted sportswoman of the century after winning 55 world cup titles, three overall championships and three Olympic gold medals.

One of the days we spent at Elm was a powder day and we could not get enough of the fresh snow. I confess I am a little biased towards Switzerland as I love the country, its people and cities and of course the magnificent landscape. The ski fields are legendary and I have never had a bad day there. Like anywhere you need time to fully appreciate a country, to get to love it and to be able to make like minded comparisons but I could easily and happily live in Switzerland.

Then I visited my good friend and fellow New Zealander Catherine Smith and her daughter Rosie who was at a ski race training camp at the Swiss resort of Adleboden - about an hour from Bern on the train. Adleboden is one of the oldest ski resorts in the world. It was founded in 1903 and was made popular by Dr Henry Lund who first and then regularly brought groups of British ski tourists to the area. Catherine's eldest daughter Taylor had been at a ski racing training camp in Austria and had recently had a nasty fall so was spending most of her time recovering in the gym and with her physio.

What I loved about Adleboden was that it was almost 100% Swiss, charming and full of atmosphere, which was actually a welcome break from Chamonix. There is a long main street full of hotels, bars, restaurants and retail all representing authentic Swiss Architecture. The skiing although very gentle in comparison to Chamonix was still very good with facilities which put it to shame.

Catherine and I worked together over 20 years ago and I happened to introduce her to her husband Ian who is one of the best skiers I have ever seen, and still regularly wins the masters race series in New Zealand. Ian would have been one of the country's foremost downhill skiers but didn't have the finances to pursue his dream, however his legacy continues happily with his children. His own family all skied together since they were very young and I have gratefully stayed at their ski house in at Mount Ruapehu for over 20 years since introducing them - it is like a second home to me.

I skied with Catherine on her first ever day on snow and took her to the very top of the mountain – it did take her sometime to forgive me. Now her two teenage daughters Taylor 18 and Rosie 15 are almost full time ski racers skiing both the full New Zealand and European winters. Hopefully they will both make the 2014 New Zealand Winter Olympics team as well as World Cup squads along the way.

You have to admire parents that go all out to support their children in a sport they love such as ski racing. Anyone that thinks a child that ski races has it easy should think again, it is unbelievably hard work and ultimately competitive. The routine is something like this. You are up at the crack of dawn every day race training; there is continuous pressure put on you from both coaches and parents to improve; after skiing you have to make sure your skis are waxed and race tuned; something that you have to do yourself; you have to maintain a high level of energy and fitness throughout the season and you have to drive all over Europe competing in races. The routine also includes biking, lifting weights, core, video analysis and physio. You have to be able to deal with accidents and injuries of which there are many in such an aggressive and dangerous sport. It is also as competitive as hell as you are racing against the very best skiers your age found anywhere in the world so you have to be prepared to lose but at the same time continually learn. And then somehow you have to catch up with your school work.

To be competitive you need to own a truck load of the latest ski equipment and two pairs of skis for each discipline that you compete in – so slalom, giant slalom and often super G skis too. You also have to pay for coaching, race entries, transport, international flights, accommodation, living costs, medical treatment, other racing equipment such as clothing, race suits, helmets and schooling too. It's not for everyone and certainly not financially accessible to many.

Taylor and Rosie continue to love the sport they excel in and have a wonderful relationship with their parents, but it is not always the case and I have witnessed many parents fulfilling their own ambitions, aspirations and dreams through their children.

A few friends of mine have represented New Zealand in downhill skiing such as Simon Wi Rutene who raced in four Olympic games and was the national champion seven times. Annelise Coberger was the first person from the Southern Hemisphere to win a medal at the winter Olympics when she won silver in 1992 in Albertville in France. I have talked to both of them about their training and it's enough to put you off skiing, which it did for both of them as they did not ski recreationally for quite a few years after they stopped competing. I question whether competing at an international level eventually does make you tire of the sport and take away the fun.

> *"It's good to ski for fun, but I still want to win races as often as possible."*
> **Hermann Maier**

The train ride back to Chamonix from Switzerland is nothing short of spectacular, breathtakingly scenic and steeped in history as the train meanders its way through a series of high altitude mountain passes – I spotted wild deer running free as the train climbs its way up the snow covered track. There is a fascinating history in these Alps and especially during wars where such geography was critical to survival. During both world wars this was one pass where thousands of allies escaped into neutral Switzerland. Thousands of people have risked their lives trying to make it through the French Alps into Switzerland and your mind boggles at the thought of it: many Jews were turned away by the Swiss or captured and tried to flee using routes such as the Haute Route which took many lives; the French resistance hid from the Germans high up in these passes and had great success during the war.

Returning to Chamonix I was blown away again by the sheer magnitude and beauty of the landscape. It's a welcoming sight.

I had told the Randoneurs Hotel where I was staying when I would be returning by scribbling the dates down - neither of the owners spoke any English. I returned to what is the busiest time in the business, half term break with all accommodation completely full, as was I with my work bookings.

It was not until a couple of days later, when I was sitting in their bar enjoying my third pint, that the English speaking French bar maid asked me when I intended to pay the bill for my stay. I casually mentioned that I had always paid my bill when I left and then found out that I had to leave in 48 hours as they were fully booked.

Unconvincingly I pleaded with her that I had asked to stay for the whole month of February but it was no use. It was times like this when I wish I had taken my French lessons a little more seriously at school. I knew Chamonix was completely booked as well and to add fuel to the fire I was cooking at a luxury chalet in the middle of town that week. Prices also sky rocketed during the busier times so I knew I would have to bite the bullet and pay top dollar for whatever I found. More importantly it also meant there would be little time to ski – bugger!

So, I then spent the next couple of days knocking on doors everywhere I could imagine. I started thinking of the movie Aspen Extreme where two friends who become ski instructors spent their first few nights in a freezing van, as sleeping in Charlie became the only obvious option.

"I have always depended on the kindness of strangers."
Tennessee Williams

That was until I knocked on the Belvédère's door - until now I had seen the sign up "Complet" – full! A Gite is like a French hostel but certainly not a youth hostel as people of all ages were welcome. If you like conviviality, exchanges and open mindedness a stay in a Gite is a very warm and cosmopolitan experience.

The first person I met was the owner Michiel, a Dutchman who has owned the Belvédère for 30 years. I breathed a sigh of fresh air when he happily told me he had one spare bed but it wouldn't be available until later. It was only when I got back very late from the Office Bar that I discovered I would be sleeping next to a rather large Scandinavian who snored gloriously - luckily the delicious alcoholic beverages I had consumed all evening were the perfect sedative to put me to sleep.

I arose early, to continuous snoring, to go and cook breakfast for my guests dreading my evening return to meet the snoring Scandinavian gentleman I had slept next to. I had no intention of staying another night but Charlie was the only other option - it was a tough choice.

To my relief Michiel shifted me to another room with three others - two of whom I would become great mates with. When I thanked him he said: "Hey, it's all part of the alpine experience". It was a statement which resounded in my head. Which is quite true, there are hundreds of mountain huts, refuges and shelters to be found throughout the Alps and often you are squeezed into a space with a bunch of other climbers due to adverse conditions, so having to top and tail is common business.

The first person I met after Michiel was a 21 year old tall and solid Northern Irishman, Patrick Mackay, whose extraordinarily friendly and outgoing personality was an instant hit with me. Patrick had loved the Indiana Jones movies so much that he completed an honours degree in archaeology but then decided he no longer wanted to be Indiana Jones so he and his girlfriend decided to spend a ski season together in Chamonix.

Unfortunately for Patrick on New Year's Day his girlfriend dumped him after three years so he ended up moving to Chamonix by himself and thus moving into the Belvédère for the duration. I think Patrick also saw coming to Chamonix as a first class opportunity to get away from his prying mother who seemed to call him at least once a day.

Patrick was intelligent, always witty and enjoyed every minute of his alpine experience. He was just the breath of fresh air I needed and our energy and synergy were contagious with the continuing flow of people we would meet, ski with, dine with, drink with, get very drunk with, and or talk to about this book.

Another room mate was Englishman Doug who had lived in Chamonix previously for around four years and had also just split up with his girlfriend in Zurich. Doug also had a very outgoing personality and when he was talking about something he loved, which mainly involved climbing and more climbing, he was impossible to stop or to get a word in edgeways for that matter. As he was watching his pennies he decided to move to a famous hut in the Argentiere hills which was aptly named The Shack.

The Shack was left vacant by the owner for skiers or climbers to live in for free and had been there for over 20 years. It was rumoured that the owner had lost his son to an accident in the Alps and the shack was some sort of reminder. Doug never stopped talking about The Shack and all of the legendary ski bums, such as Trevor Petersen or Seth Morrison, who once lived there. The Shack was nestled in hidden trees somewhere up in the hills at the back of the village and you had to be invited to visit by someone who had previously stayed there - it all sounded a bit weird to me like some sort of ski bums' members club or cult.

Not knowing where it was and at 4.00am in the morning after a monolithic night at The Office, Patrick and I decided to go and visit Doug at The Shack. Well, we eventually found it by chance but Doug was still out on the town and it was a nightmare walking the steep uphill track through deep snow in a pitch black forest and not knowing where the hell we were going. I got very lost on the way, as did Patrick, who had decided to give up and sleep in the deep snow, but we eventually found it by following footprints in the snow – I also could smell the smoke from the log fire. Once we found it we discovered that The Shack is a wonderful spot and the atmosphere like a high altitude mountain hut.

Our other roommate was 30 year old Dermot who was from Dublin complete with an accent which sounded like Brad Pitt in Snatch. Dermott was fired from his IT job in Ireland and decided to come to Chamonix. I am not sure why he got fired from his job as all he seemed to do apart from eat was play on his computer. He was also obsessed with mountain climbing and his bed had ropes, karabiners, ice screws and the like hanging from it. I think it was supposed to give him the feeling he was sleeping on the side of a steep cliff while mountain climbing or something like that. Well we never saw or heard of him doing any climbing but every few days or so he would rearrange his gear. He reminded me of Dustin Hoffman's character in Rain Man. Each to their own, I am sure there are thousands like him out there for whom just owning the gear is as exciting as doing it.

The Belvédère slept 50 and turned over 2000 guests a year and it turned out to be the perfect place to research and continue writing this book. It is in a unique and somewhat quaint looking building. You know when you are at school and you draw your first house with more than one story, well it looks like that.

There were no surrounding structures so its four stories stood out from the crowd and were very noticeable when driving past. Rooms on the Mont Blanc side also had balconies where there were stunning views from every angle. There were guests from every country imaginable - Russia, Eastern Europe, Japan. Korea, China, all over Scandinavia, all over Europe, the USA, Canada and Australasia - in fact everywhere, anywhere and all walks of life and no one was ever out of place or didn't fit in.

The Belvédère was also only a quick walk across the road to the Grand Montets ski field and just five minutes to the local bars in Argentiere. The kitchen was large, open plan and the dining room seated just over 50 people. Once a restaurant too, it had a commercial kitchen downstairs with a dumb waiter to bring up the food. It also had a very good sauna! When the dining room was full it hummed like a busy restaurant full of cheer and song.

I became marvellous friends with Kiki who managed the Gite – a fireball of a French woman, she had lived in Chamonix for seven years and had previously lived in London for 17 year and Paris before that. She both telemarked and alpine skied with tremendous speed and with no sign of fear, like many do that started the sport very young. She knew everybody in the valley and introduced me to many of the people I have interviewed for this book. She had a heart of gold, but God help you if you got on the wrong side of her - her staunchness could scare even the most fearless!

I met a tonne of people staying at the Gite and could easily fill a book with them alone. There was Sue Roberts who moved into our room for a couple of weeks and then returned to stay for the last three. Sue had built up a successful career in Public Relations but had experienced enough of the stress and the shallow people she had spent many years working with. She had also been motivated to come to Chamonix by recently losing her mother with whom she was extraordinarily close. The two combined put everything into perspective so she decided to quit and have a season Chamonix - which she never looked back on. Sue managed a rental apartment during the season and came and stayed at the Belvédère when it was full - which was often the case. Sue was a top-notch person to bounce my many ideas off for the book to the extent that she decided to do the PR for what you are reading.

I can and will say many positive things about the Gite but one thing it lacked was any hint of sophistication and Sue and I would try and redress the balance by drinking Champagne (well a damned good method) after skiing.

> *"We should come home from adventures and perils, and discoveries every day with new experience and character."*
> **Henry David Thoreau 1817-1862**

The Belvédère was a melting-pot for many other eccentrics who were for some reason or another attracted to the lifestyle that the Gite offered. I almost called this chapter "One Flew Over the Cuckoo's Nest" due to how much of a disequilibrium the Gite would often be, but that's what made it so great.

There are many who warrant a mentioned and at the top of my list is American Mark Corville. Put him in an Italian suit and he would look and definitely sound like a character out of Good Fellas. Mark, as far as I know, is the world's oldest living ski bum, clocking in at just under 60 years old. He has skied since he was three and never done much of anything else.

Mark started skiing in Stowe Vermont in the USA where he was raised and then became a professional skier - to this day he still gets his ski gear for free. He came to Chamonix eight years ago as it's the best in the world he confidently says. He has been living at the Belvédère for seven years where he helps clean to pay his rent.

He rarely misses a day on the slopes and the only reason he does is if the mountain is closed or according to him should be. Over the years Mark had skied professionally with most of the legendary skiers of the past half century and Kikki said he was known to be one of the best five skiers in the entire Chamonix valley.

I had mixed sentiments about Mark's lifestyle. Certainly he was as eccentric as anyone I had ever met, but he decided long ago that what he enjoyed the most in life was skiing and being the very best he could be at it was his buzz. As he had done little else in life the question I asked myself was had he missed out on what else it has to offer? It would be hard to meet a more passionate skier anywhere - Mark just took the extreme to the extreme. He seemed very content with his life if not a little lonely and man did he love to talk skiing.

His daily routine consisted of getting up at about 6.00am, having breakfast then catching the 7.15 am bus to Les Houches where he would wait half an hour at the bus stop before being the very first on the lift. He would then mono ski or telemark for up to three hours and catch the bus home. He would then make lunch and walk the dog before waxing his skis or mono board to perfection. Next he would spend three hours on his static bike religiously watching eighties ski movies such as the Blizzard of AAHHH'S which was a hit when his skiing was peaking. He would then have dinner before going to bed and watching more eighties ski movies until he fell asleep. He would then get up and do exactly the same thing the next day.

Mark was renowned in the valley for his crazy straight lining - simply pointing your skis downhill and skiing a straight line the entire length of the ski slope - certainly not for the faint hearted and you can only do it on a slope where there are no other people. Mark said: "Well you know John, you can only straight line for a limited time during the season; the beginning of the season is best and it has to be where there are no other skiers at all." Well if you are skiing close to 160km you had better make sure there is no one in front of you.

During the summer Mark would hop on his mountain bike and head of in search of new couloirs to ski, dreaming of the mountains being open, dreaming of what that piste would be like to conquer. What I also liked about Mark was that he enjoyed watching his skiing progress and get better and noticed continual improvements every season. Mark concluded that technology helped: "But, John, you know you can always push yourself that little bit harder, and pushing your fear harder is a lot of fun."

The Gite soon became like a home with a very large extended family where you entertained daily - it was like throwing a dinner party for friends every night. There were a bunch of us that would cook together every evening and usually we would invite new travellers to join us. I was always astounded by the people I met there from all walks of life but all engulfed by the spirit of the mountains and Chamonix especially.

The Belvédère had a regular clientele as well as many who had mostly heard about the place through word of mouth. Michiel did not do any advertising at all for the Gite as it would not attract his target market made up mostly of hard core skiers, boarders, climbers, ski tourers etc.

The formula worked well and considering how eclectic the mix there were rarely delays in using the kitchen or the showers.

"A man's growth is seen in the successive choirs of his friends."
Ralph Waldo Emerson

Many of the guests were regulars who came back year after year, some had worked at the Belvédère previously or had, at some stage, spent a season or two or five in the valley. Every night stories would unfold about previous adventures, storms, accidents and of course death. Michiel made it quite clear to me that anyone who lives in the valley comes to accept death as part of the lifestyle here. Over the 30 years he has owned the Belvédère close to a dozen people who were staying at the Gite have lost their lives pursuing some sort of alpine adventure.

The Belvédère also attracted people of all ages. Towards the end of my stay there was a 16 year old couple Smelliot and Leonie who were staying there by themselves. They were madly in love and their youthful and ebullient energy was a hit with us all and they would often socialise with us until very late in the morning. Don't you think a couple of 16 year old school students having a romantic holiday in the French Alps is wonderful?

At the other end of the age scale was John a 60 something who had spent his career as a Formula One mechanic and, as he had spent a lot of time in Japan, we dubbed Jap John. He was an English gentleman and just turned up at the Gite like I had, fitted in splendidly and never left. He was also a marvellous cook producing superb roast dinners and especially talented at baking - making his own pastry and wonderful pies. His passion was also extended to red wine and we finished off many a bottle making nonsensical conversation until the small hours.

Jap John was as eccentric as anyone I had ever met - he is a walking encyclopaedia of anything mechanical, exotic or racing car related. He doesn't ski, but is still living at the Belvédère where he spends much of his time designing race cars. I left Charlie in his good hands when he wouldn't start when I left Chamonix.

There was also Englishman Pistol Pete and his French girlfriend Cecile who met skiing at La Tour. Pete a few years older than me had skied and instructed all over the world and now spends most of his ski time with the beautiful Cecile ski touring. They rented an apartment on the top floor of the Gite but always cooked and ate in the dining room. I skied the Vallée Blanche with Pete and Aleid and thus the name Pistol Pete as his skiing was that perfect.

Aleid was an attractive 35 year old Dutch doctor who had been coming to the Belvédère for many years, which sadly included time to recover from cancer. Chamonix and the Belvédère was thus a very special place for her. She had completed a PHD and her studies included all sorts of tests on post traumatic cold intolerance in median and ulnar nerve injury. She insisted that she put my hand in freezing cold water for half an hour to see how it affected me. No way Jose!

When we skied the Vallée Blanche together she spent two hours testing total strangers' blood oxygen content when they had just arrived at 3,812 metres while Pistol Pete and I waited patiently and our perfect day beckoned. These sort of experiments started way back in 1820 when Doctor Joseph Hamel led a fatal expedition to Mont Blanc as he wanted to observe the effects of high altitude. When I asked for some basic information on what her thesis was all about she sent me notes that would fill a library. She was crazy, but very likeable, and probably the most passionate woman skier I have ever met - she was just mad about skiing.

> *"Friendship is unnecessary, like philosophy, like art...It has no survival value; rather it is one of those things that give value to survival."*
> **C. S. Lewis**

Two of the most fun people I met at the Belvédère were Jules and Jimbo. These guys had the best job in the world as they sold Buffs to every possible ski resort. You know those things you have around your neck to keep it warm, or around your head or whatever.

Jules was skiing the Vallée Blanche about 12 years ago and someone had fallen down a crevasse and after rescuing the person and probably saving their life, he was offered the European franchise for Buff – which has since expanded to become a global business and you would be hard pressed to find a ski resort that doesn't stock them.

I was envious of how much he got to travel and with such a unique product. His own company is called Sue Me which he initiated when he fell out with a crook of a business partner. The company's philosophy is based on what goes around come around and on utilising organic and sustainable materials.

There were literally hundreds of others staying at the Gite I really enjoyed meeting such as Aussie Joe the kick boxer and his sensational Dutch girlfriend Miriam. They had rented a small apartment in the Belvédère for six weeks. Miriam was similar to Aleid in that she was crazy about snowboarding to the extent she wanted to do little else in her life. She had spent the previous season as a chalet manager and after six weeks in Chamonix was considering doing it all over again.

The last person I will mention was another Englishman, Dave. Dave was retired and once a passionate mountain climber and had sumitted Mont Blanc amongst many other peaks. He was a little short on funds this season so did not ski and like Mark helped out at the Gite for his accommodation. Dave seemed to know every last bit of history in the valley and was a big help to me. He would often sip his cup of tea on the Belvédère balcony peering at Mont Blanc with an airy look of satisfaction like they were old friends.

Most people stayed at the Gite because it was inexpensive but many stayed like Jules, Sue or me as it was a phenomenal way to meet people and to fully enjoy the alpine experience. You could cook there, socialise and entertain, sit on the deck and look at sensational views of Mont Blanc, there was also plenty of parking. I loved it because there was a continuous flow of some of the most interesting people I had ever met and I beg to differ but staying in a two to five stay hotel is not nearly as interesting or as social. Well there is an argument about good linen and a hot bath but...

When you travel anywhere on this planet your fondest memories are usually of the people you meet and in this regard the Belvédère provided exactly that. It is the sort of place you can return to in five, ten or 15 years time and know you will bump into some of the same friendly faces which is rare. It's a home away from home but in the stunning French Alps.

"If civilisation is to survive, we must cultivate the science of human relationships – the ability of all peoples, of all kinds, to live together, in the same world at peace."
Franklin D. Roosevelt

Chapter Ten
Chamonix's tragic history

"A healthy human environment is one in which we try to make sense of our limits, of the accidents that can always befall us and the passage of time which inexorably changes us."
Rowan Williams

I was in two minds whether to include this chapter as human beings we are not really conditioned to deal with death. But after spending the whole winter in Chamonix there was hardly a week that went past that you did not hear of a death in the valley if not a serious accident. It is very much part of the alpine experience and has also helped shape Chamonix into the world famous status it now enjoys.

There has been an underlying theme to date about risk verses pleasure throughout this book and what some people are prepared to do to feel their best on the mountain. What astounded me is just how dangerous the area is for all that venture into the Chamonix valley. I hope this chapter leaves you thinking a little more about risk and what you individually consider your limits. I know it has helped me understanding my own. It has often been said that people who regularly take big risks in the mountains must be considered either profoundly selfish or incapable of sympathy for those who love them.

Writing a book like this I was also possibly privy to hearing about some of the significant tragic events perhaps a little more than most. The French/European/UK media as you would or would not expect are obsessed with death in the Alps as it sells newspapers, magazines and gets people glued to their televisions and laptops. On the other hand the Chamonix mountain management underplay death for obvious reasons as it is no good for tourism. I tend to disagree as firstly there is no such thing as bad publicity and also every experienced and probably intermediate skier in the world has heard of Chamonix and anyone with half a brain has heard of Mount Blanc.

"Nowhere in the world are the risks and the rewards of a life in the mountains revealed more clearly than in the valley of Chamonix."
STEEP

You would have an easier job holding back the tide than stopping the adventurous from coming to Chamonix and if the tourism office stopped spending a cent they would still all come. I would also suggest that many who come are more than familiar with its reputation with well known terms being thrown around calling the area the death sport capital of the world.

It would be easy to write a series of books on death in the valley. Mont Blanc alone has taken over 1000 lives. Think of all the pain and hurt these people have caused their families just by seeking a higher adventure for their own pleasure and I am sure the eulogy at each funeral was similar, "Well he/she died doing what they love." Of course no one wants to die but death is just something that goes hand-in-hand with this ski resort more than any other in the world. The reason is simply, because people push their limits, their fear barriers and their confidence more in Chamonix more than anywhere else.

Of course that is a bit of a generalisation but the statistics are there to prove it. I also witnessed a monumental amount of accidents. It was unbelievable, broken legs, brain damage, collar bones, backs, ribs to name a few and every time I drove someone to one of the many hospitals in the area they were full to the brim. I concluded that accidents happen more in Chamonix once again because of the extreme off piste skiing that is more readily available here. The town simply attracts the experienced skier who, like me, has previously pushed most of the boundaries available. But, also like me, your skiing experience elsewhere does not make you necessarily ready to tackle the skiing in Chamonix which extends as far as the eye can see and beyond.

**"Skiing is the only sport where you spend an arm and a leg
to break an arm and a leg."**
Anon

So, people learn the hard way and you can't blame them for it. I was lucky during the season as I had half a dozen falls at speed off piste and was fortunate enough to walk away with a little bruising.

There is not a day in Chamonix where you do not see or hear a helicopter pass by and as heli skiing is banned in France they are most likely doing rescues. There are on average 700 winter helicopter rescues – one third in the Vallée Blanche alone.

The scariest moment of my time in Chamonix was when I was skiing down a very steep vertical drop out of the back of the Grand Montets. I had a perfect line in one day old deep powder snow. I fell once and landed on my head and shoulder and then got back up not thinking too much about it - as you often do when the adrenalin diminishes any elements of fear.

The run was coming to an end and I needed to pick up speed to cut the line through a very steep cliff face to make it across to another slope to finish the run to the bottom. I then took another fall just a minute of two after the first. This time I clipped my edge and came out of my skis and fell easily 50 meters or so sliding down the steep slope. Patrick was skiing behind me and got my skis for me, he had a look of bewilderment on his face as I was completely covered in snow and he expected that I had hurt myself.

We looked at where we had to ski and he confidently took the lead and made it across the cliff face with ease. Both times I should have waited and regained composure and momentum but, foolhardy as it was I continued and, sub-consciously, lacking confidence I did not pick up enough speed. I got stuck on the side of the icy cliff face causing me to almost free fall another 40 meters - and then what would have been a fast slide down another 100 metres or more onto the next steep slope. In fear my body was completely shaking as I started to slide down the rock hard icy steep face. All I could do was fling my arms out to try and get a grip with the other end of my ski poles which by then I was using like ice axes.

I was just hanging there like Tom Cruise in the start of Mission Impossible. Then I dug my ski edges in as deeply as possible and slowing made my way across the pitch by hugging the snow like a teddy bear and rolling over to the other side. Patrick was about ten metres down the slope clearly buzzing from his own adventurous crossing. "Man that was some wild traverse huh:" he said with his eyes pulsating. Yes you could say that again! If I had lost my grip and slid a meter further I was a gonner and god only knows what would have happened to me. Those few minutes were as scary as I have ever had on skis - even more scary than my mountain climb at high school. It was a lesson in getting your momentum back as well as your confidence, especially after a couple of falls. The next hour or so I was in a state of shock and decided to call it a day and headed to the sauna at the Gite to heal my sore muscles.

I have had many accidents over the years but have never broken a bone but Christ I have been lucky. I have fallen off cliffs in-between large rocks and as I had a broken arm at the time I put my arm out to slow me down and it took my cask clean off cutting up my broken arm in the process. It was difficult explaining to the doctor what exactly had happened when he re-casked my arm.

Another accident happened when I was training for a multi sport event about ten years ago. Individually you had to ski 4 km, mountain bike 36km, road cycle 35km, white water kayak 17km, water ski 32km and then run 12km to the finish and all in one day non-stop as fast as you could go. The event was called the Crater to the Lake as it started from the crater of a living volcano on Mount Ruapehu in New Zealand and finished at the end of New Zealand's largest lake, Lake Taupo.

During training for this event I was doing a long distance run around the steep sea cliffs of Wellington in New Zealand where I lived at the time. I hurt my ankle on the rocks and slowed down. When it got dark I took a wrong turn and to cut a long story short ended up on a perpendicular rock face in the pitch black as I was trying to take a short cut to save time.

So there I was, like in Chamonix, stuck on a cliff face thinking if I fall I die. It was the middle of winter and my only option to survive was to jump about 20 metres down into the freezing sea in between sharp facing rocks. It was scary as all hell but my thoughts were tuned to how on earth I was going to get out of this situation. So I jumped and fell into the frigid water (I fell through ice into a pond once and it did not seem this bloody cold).

Ideally, I should have climbed up but it was way too steep, way too dark and one slip and I would break my back in the fall. So I jumped not knowing exactly how deep it was as the large waves crashed over my body. I made it to the shore devastated that I had to make my way round what looked like a couple of hundred metres of more steep rock faces. To this day I have never felt as cold and I kept having to go back into the freezing water to swim when the rock faces got too steep to traverse.

My hands were bleeding badly from gripping the rocks as I eventually made it to a beach where an old nemesis just happened to be fishing in the distance. I could not even run as my entire body was totally numb - like when you get a dead leg but all over - but they were jut leaving. They just happened to hear my feeble yells and it was my old rival business owner who gave me a lift. (We had both owned horse riding schools and never got on, but bloody hell was I pleased to see him as it started to bucket down with chilling rain.)

Later in the week I invited him and his family to my restaurant where a mutual penchant for red wine was discovered and we have been friends ever since. After visiting my doctor I was told that I was most likely suffering second stage hypothermia due to the length of time I spent in the water and because of how I reacted to it physically. The freezing water caused a dramatic increase in my heart rate, blood pressure and breathing rate which was especially dangerous as I had been running for a few hours in little clothing and my body temperature went from one extreme to the other. Your body temperature is about 36 – 37.2 degrees Celsius and if this falls to below 35 you will be suffering from hypothermia and are in serious trouble. Serious meaning you will probably die within the hour. Even though you lose heat 27 times faster in water than you do on land hypothermia has killed many skiers in the Alps and something you should be prepared for, especially when touring.

In regards to ski accidents I have had many but I have been lucky and it will never stop me pursuing sports that I love. I have witnessed firsthand hundreds of accidents like one of the first school ski trips I went on where a class mate broke both legs in front of me. I mention my accidents as they are all part of the alpine experience, when you ski as much as I have you accept that they are going to happen and the risks increase the more you push yourself. Ask any extreme skier and they will tell you the risks are worth it and I agree totally with that.

The day I skied the Vallée Blanche the slope on Mont Blanc where eight climbers were killed on August 2008, was pointed out to me. They were all experienced climbers from Switzerland and Austria and there was an avalanche which caused them to fall between 1000 and 1500 meters to their deaths. It's a strange feeling when you have been close to that exact spot.

The worst avalanche in the Chamonix Valley happened on the ninth of February 1999. It had snowed heavily for four days. The avalanche happened in the village of Montroc which is nestled at the bottom of the La Tour ski field. It was the biggest avalanche in 40 years. There were 300,000 cubic meters of snow channelled directly onto the hamlet below and nothing could resist these massive forces of nature. Travelling at 60 mph chalets were pulverised and the debris carried over 100 meters. When it finally stopped 14 buildings had been destroyed and six seriously damaged. The remains and any people inside were buried under 100,000 tonnes of snow to a depth of five meters. It was like a bomb had been dropped in the whole area. In total 12 people died including four children whilst 20 people, including eight children, were pulled out alive.

It was a corrupt official who took a bribe almost 40 years ago to change the avalanche zoning maps allowing construction to infrequent through obviously dangerous avalanche paths. Four years later the Mayor of Chamonix Michel Charlet was found guilty of second degree murder and received a three month suspended sentence. As you can imagine there was an uproar - modern technology should have predicted this happen.

"Life is a gamble. You can get hurt, but people die in plane crashes, lose their arms and legs in car accidents; people die every day. Same with fighters: some die, some get hurt, some go on. You just don't let yourself believe it will happen to you."
Muhammad Ali

There have been some horrific years when people were killed by avalanches such as 1916 when 3000 Austrian troops were killed in the Italian Dolomites; the winter of 1951 when 265 people were killed in Austria and Switzerland alone; 1970 when 39 people died in Val d' Isere and another 37 were injured. 74 more died that year, 56 of them children in Plateau d Assy. and as recently as the winter of 2008 100 people were killed in avalanches including eight on Mont Blanc.

My friend Paul Holding, who I shared a room at the Belvédère later in the season, has a popular blog, The Adventures of A Spilt Boarder (www. theadventuresofasplitboarder.com) and is an example of many extreme skiers (or in his case boarders) who come to Chamonix.

Paul has a snow board that splits so he can walk up mountains with skins and then board down. What he and his extreme minded friends get up to is madness in my books but definitely not in his. He often climbs and then boards in place where you can put a foot wrong and fall to your death. He also went on a ski tour in the States when he ended up having to build a snow cave as he could not make the decent required that day due to the weather turning really nasty. He ended up with frost bite on his toes which I can tell you is excruciatingly painful - especially if someone like me steps on your foot by mistake.

When I asked Paul about the risks associated with the limits he pushes he said: "Risk is purely perception, we always calculate the risks anyway. Everyone seems to have an opinion on what other people do with their lives and it's none of their business." Paul is one of tens of thousands of adventure thrill seekers that come to Chamonix and the risk is as much of the draw of the card as the actual skiing.

People die every year in the mountains due to freezing, falling, avalanches, starvation, exhaustion, rock fall, ice-fall and altitude sickness.

As well as death however, there are amazing survival stories. One of the most legendary happened on August 17th 1934 when Guy Labor survived eight days in a crevasse that he fell into. This happening inspired a novel by Chamonix mountain guide and author Roger Frison-Roche called La Grand Crevasse. There have been thousands of successful rescues of a similar nature throughout the valley's history.

1999 was the worst year possible for Chamonix in modern times. Not only was there an horrific avalanche in Montroc, but there was also a fire in the Mont Blanc tunnel. I mention it for two reasons, one because it could and should never have happened and also because one brave Italian risked all to save others. There is a gold monument at the tunnel's entrance on the Chamonix side and this thought provoking disaster is a nasty reminder of Chamonix's tragic history.

On the 24th March 1999 just over a month after the avalanche in Montroc a Belgian transport truck carrying flour and margarine caught fire in the tunnel. As cars flashed their lights at the driver he soon realised something was wrong. This was not yet a fire emergency as there had been 16 other truck fires in the tunnel over the previous 35 years – they were always extinguished on the spot by the drivers. The 57 year old driver stopped and attempted to put out the growing flames erupting from his cab. A few minutes later tunnel employees triggered the fire alarm and stopped all future traffic from entering. There were ten cars/vans and 18 trucks already in the tunnel. Some cars managed to turn round while others either sat in their cars and waited for help with their windows rolled up or made a run for it, but the ventilation system backed down the tunnel faster than anyone could run to safety.

The fumes quickly filled the tunnel causing vehicle engines to stall. The tunnel acted like a chimney sucking in cold air on one side with the intense heat and smoke leaving on the other. In total 27 people died in their vehicles and ten died trying to escape on foot. Of the 50 people initially trapped by the fire only 12 survived. Pielucio Tinazzi an Italian security guard is credited with saving ten of the 12 survivors by riding his motorbike into the inferno. Sadly as the heat intensified he succumbed and perished too. The tunnel was closed for three years and there was a major international court case where once again the Mayor of Chamonix, amongst a large group of others, was put on trial for manslaughter. I talked to many people about 1999 and it is something all would rather forget. I say this not as there is something to be learnt by it all, but so it never happens again.

As I have said throughout this book, if you documented deaths and serious accidents in Chamonix over the last 100 years, there are thousands of horrific stories that could be told that would fill a library. During world war two there were many confrontations and battles fought in the Chamonix Valley and many deaths and accidents happened as a result. Can you imagine what it must have been like fighting on steep slopes, on the glaciers, below seracs and across crevasses wondering every time a bomb exploded whether you would survive the oncoming avalanches?

Chamonix undoubtedly attracts a certain breed of person who is not as worried as much about risk and danger as the average individual – so, it is perhaps just a matter of numbers and luck as to when their time is up!

Spending a full season in Chamonix created a much deeper awareness and appreciation of the dangers of all alpine pursuits. It also instilled in me, I think more caution when tackling new slopes especially in fresh snow. I will continue to take risks in the mountains but just how much risk is indeed an open question.

Chapter Eleven
Developing responsible tourism in Chamonix

"The sun, the moon, the stars would have disappeared long ago had they happened to be within the reach of predatory human hands."
Havelock Ellis

I thought it important to look forward, what future lies ahead for Chamonix, its economy and tourism growth but more importantly for me sustainability, responsible tourism and environmental issues. I have to admit to having been a complete consumer of the environment, hardly a contributor at all and remember in my youth viewing the likes of Greenpeace as nothing more than a bunch of hippies.

I am appalled by the pollution I have seen in Europe, especially the Mediterranean sea which is nothing more than a large tip, it's disgusting, not to mention the likes of the USA or China. The more I see of the world the more disappointed am in what is happening to the environment. Luckily the movement towards environmental redemption is a growing one and I was to find out Chamonix Mont Blanc is a good example of this.

I take my hat off to environmentalists and what I have seen in my lifetime is enough to easily motivate me to do whatever I can to make a difference in the preservation of our environment, starting with the simple things such as recycling, addressing my carbon footprint and other issues such as wild life and plant survival.

Environmental issues such as global warming are at the forefront of national and international concern. I was blown away witnessing firsthand how quickly the glaciers are shrinking in the Chamonix valley. It's not too dissimilar to the Native American Indians as they witnessed thousands and thousands of bison being slaughtered for their furs. It produced the biggest change the American environment had ever seen and once the bison were gone the Indians soon followed and so the pattern continues as man destroys almost everything.

> ***"Take nothing but pictures, leave nothing but footprints, kill nothing but time."***

Having interviewed local tourism and government offices I was provided with enough information to write an entire book on responsible tourism in the valley – thankfully others have beaten me to it – but I'm thankful that measures are being taken to ensure the future of this unbelievably beautiful part of our world.

Coming from New Zealand, where we have some of the highest environmental standards found anywhere in the world, it was reassuring to see that the Chamonix authorities are firmly focused on the protection of the valley without overtly limiting access to it – undoubtedly a difficult balancing act.

Part of the pressure of course has been caused by the very quick shift from agro-pastoral activities to tourism and leisure as well as the growth in international travel which has enabled the rapid increase in visitor numbers who now flock to the valley every year. Can you imagine the environmental impact of more than five million visitors year has on the valley?

With year round tourism now playing such a huge part in the economic well being of the commune, preservation of the landscape and natural resources which attract those visitors is without doubt vital if the area is to continue to flourish.

Chamonix's focus is on establishing balance between areas of intensive infrastructure – the town, housing, lifts and other infrastructure and those without.

Despite its magnificent appearance, the Chamonix area is very fragile, subject to climate evolutions and to the pressures of mass human activity. It is encouraging to know that when you visit that there are thousands of people whether on a professional, philanthropic or volunteer basis are very conscious of the stakes in years to come.

Chamonix is not alone in valuing Mont Blanc and the massif that surrounds it. It has joined forces with 35 different communes from

Switzerland, Italy and France under the banner Espace Mont Blanc in a mission is to protect this natural wonder of the world.

That's not to say that it doesn't take a very local approach to environmental issues too, despite, in my view, some shortcomings to it, there is an integrated and extensive environmentally friendly transport system. There is also active support for alpine farmers and the local tourism office is leading from the front – achieving the international environmental management standard ISO14001 in 2008. They recognise that environmental responsibility today forms part of the choice criteria for many visitors to the valley.

I am please to conclude in this brief chapter that Chamonix is doing everything possible to protect nature and the biodiversity of the living heritage. They are increasing the number of actions to protect local wildlife, conservation of natural sites, demarcation of animal hibernation areas, management of forests, development of agritourism and local produce, monitoring the climate and ecosystems, stringently managing water as well as educating the very young about sustainable development by initiating educational programmes.

Espace Mont Blanc meanwhile is focused on encouraging integrated tourism and ensuring that economic development and environmental protection go hand in hand. I've been privileged to spend time in this magnificent landscape and knowing what futures lies in store leaves me with a wonderful feeling of contentment as well as respect for these local active authorities.

"Take care of the earth and she will take care of you."

Chapter Twelve
Goodbye Chamonix Mont Blanc, but not for long

"How lucky am I to have something that makes saying goodbye so hard."
Carol Sobieski and Thomas Meehan - Annie

I left Chamonix at the end of April as I had been offered an excellent job in Nice as head chef at an Australian restaurant. The skiing was still first-class as it snows quite often in April but you have to get up there quickly as once it gets warm the fresh snow changes speedily as the sun softens it.

I had spent a lot of time in the south of France and thought it would be the perfect place to unwind, gather my thoughts and finish this book which is exactly what I am doing right now. I found a perfect apartment on the south side of the old town with a study to write in and I can hear the waves crashing as I go to sleep with the warm sea breeze flowing into my bedroom.

When I walk to work I have a choice of routes: through the old town where there are fruit and vegetable markets every day and where Matisse's old studio hovers at the end of the walkway; or I can walk around the coast with its stunning sea views, past the vast array of luxury motor yachts to the old port until I reach the Kookaburra restaurant where I am working.

It is far from the world of high Alps, adventure and snow capped mountains but it's the perfect place to reflect and finish this book. There is not a day that goes by after a full season on the mountains when all you want to do when you get up is put on your ski boots and head for the slopes. It is moments like that when you pinch yourself for having potentially been a little complacent at times during the season.

> *"As social beings we live with our eyes upon reflection, but have no assurance of the tranquillity of the waters in which we see it."*
> **Charles Horton Cooley**

A week before I was due to leave Chamonix, Charlie would not start. It was as if he was asking me "are you MAD? Why would you want to leave Chamonix, it's a field of dreams, what could be better than this?" Perhaps, but I needed to find a way to continue to fund my writing habit so the south of France was where I was headed - with or without Charlie.

It was a surprisingly sad day when I said goodbye to everyone at the Gite. I was wrestling with a rather large hangover as we had all gone out the night before. Towards the end of the season it seems like every night is a farewell party for some seasonaire or another, just like the beginning is full of opening parties.

Sue drove me to Saint Gervais which is about half an hour's drive away. Chamonix laid it on for me with perfect weather and crystal blue skies as we drove out of the gateway of Europe's largest mountain and down the yellow brick road. Without even realising it there were tears rolling-down my face which I quickly tried to hide from Sue.

> *"Don't be dismayed with goodbyes. A farewell is necessary before you can meet again. And meeting again, after moments or lifetimes* is certain for those who are friends."*
> **Richard Bach**

Saint Gervais is a beautiful old alpine town and seeing it for the first time I was disappointed I had not spent more time there. All season and for many years I had wanted to see Val d'Isere which is usually about a three and a half hour drive from Chamonix but without Charlie the only way to get there was to hitch-hike - so that was what I did.

I waited about ten minutes before I got a lift to Megève which is about 45 minutes from Chamonix. It is a stunning very up market ski resort which was built from scratch by Baroness de Rothschild. She used to frequent St Moritz until the Great War broke out. She set up her house in Paris as a hospital and went to spend a much deserved break in neutral Switzerland in 1916. To her horror she found it to be swarming with Germans. So she built France's first purpose built ski resort.

From Megeve I got a lift almost immediately all the way to Val d'Isere with two Swedish blokes who had been driving their Volvo non-stop for 28 hours from Stockholm. There is a famous mountain pass you can take through the Alps. First you have to drive through the Mont Blanc tunnel and then over the Italian Alps into the French Alps and then into Val d'Isere – well, they should have checked that the pass was open and had to drive all the way back through the tunnel and around the long way which of course is not cheap!

Their misfortune was my good fortune however, as they gave me a lift to the hotel where I stayed for a few nights. The drive from Chamonix to Val d'Isere is sensational as you pass through a constant flow of ski resorts and towns such as Albertville where the 1992 Winter Olympics were staged. The town of Bourg Saint Maurice is also spectacular about half an hour before you get to Val d'Isere – and it's a mind bogglingly gigantic ski area. It's somewhere I have long heard about and wanted to ski – with more than 300km of groomed trails alone, all there is for as far as the eye can see are pistes.

After 50 nights at the Gite the highlight for me - which ranked alongside the skiing - was booking into a good hotel: crisp linen, satellite TV and the luxury of my own bathroom complete with the best selection of toiletries I'd seen in quite a while. A gallon of bubbles and a bottle of wine were the perfect accompaniment to my reflections on a season well spent.

However both Val d'Isere, and the connected resort of Tignes, has some appalling architecture – the result of architects who, as far as I am concerned, took way too much acid in the sixties. There are high rises all over the vicinity that you would expect to see in New York not a ski resort.

I had a couple of weeks skiing at Correncon en Vercors and Villard de Lans near Grenoble, a couple of years ago where the 1968 Winter Olympics were held and I found the same monstrosities there. These buildings take so much away from the beauty of the landscape and the stunning mountain backdrop.

In Val d'Isere I was told that they had spent close to 100 million Euros to give them a much needed face lift. On a positive note there are some stunning chalets mainly made of the local stone throughout the area and the town itself is very upmarket.

Anyway it was an entirely appropriate way to finish my very first full winter ski season in Europe. Looking back over the last five months I had an enormous amount of gratitude for so many things. I had made: some outstanding new friends that I knew I would keep in touch with and hopefully catch up with on the slopes again and lifelong friends that I would always have a deeper connection with. I had met some incredible people who live and have a fantastic lifestyle full of adventure and excitement that I admired. I learnt to ski off piste with confidence and expertise and had many of the best days on skis I have ever had. My cooking had progressed even further and at the end of the season I treated myself to a full set of German Zwilling, Henckels chef's knives. I surprised myself with how well my skiing progressed and have the ski bug as much as I ever have.

Socially Chamonix's hospitality was always there to keep me stimulated and entertained on just about every level. I learnt as much as I could in five months about this marvellous place, its history, its food and wine, the chalet business, the culture, its sustainable future and all that jazz.

Sure I thrived on information overload but everyday presented me with something new and unique. I loved the progression of Chamonix's changing season and its impact on the mountains: all hell freezing over and totally bitter cold in December with hard frosts and lots of ice; a reminder to keep your skis finely tuned especially sharpened edges; January's virgin snow coming on a regular basis whilst it remained intensely cold with white-outs and brilliant powder days. The persistent snow flurries and heavy falls in February with knee deep powder skiing. Three weeks of surprisingly hot sunshine in March carving up the corn snow. Finally, warm spring like weather in April wearing often only a tea-shirt but with immense surprise snowstorms coming and going on a regular basis.

Chamonix takes on a new life in April as all the snow melts and the poor council workers have a massive job cleaning up five months of dog poop emerging from the melted snow. On a more positive note every café, restaurant and bar puts tables outside, gelatos goes on sale on every corner and the street atmosphere completely changes – along with street fashion which quickly changes too.

What I love especially about mountain weather is how altogether unpredictable it is and thus it continually surprises you and Chamonix did not disappoint.

What I will always be most appreciative for is how I personally developed throughout this time. What I have not really touched on is the amount of time it was just me and Chamonix, whether it was driving Charlie around in a snow storm, shopping for clients, the incredulously early morning starts, skiing by myself a great deal - like I did on Christmas day - or the many hours I spent alone on a ski lift as I was either first on or last off.

I am thankful that I had this time to reflect and to put everything in my life back into perspective. Life is so damn short and before we know it we will be sitting in a rocking chair looking back remembering the best time of our lives and Chamonix's gift to me was my perfect transition to the extent where I had to be talked into letting anyone else read what I have written.

> *"Somebody should tell us, right at the start of our lives, that we are dying. Then we might live life to the limit, every minute of every day. Do it! I say. Whatever you want to do, do it now! There are only so many tomorrows."*
> **Michael Landon**

That quote has always motivated me to ski more. After one winter season in Chamonix I feel I have only just touched the surface and in no way am I pertaining to be an expert on Chamonix.

This book is just about what I did, saw, heard, read, ate, drank, watched and researched. Everything I did and ventured was all part of the alpine experience that you could personally experience at a number of acclaimed ski resorts. There is plenty I have left out and many people that probably warrant a mention that I have not included but I had to draw the line somewhere. I could have spent the next five or ten years speaking to experts in all the fields and subject matter I have covered that's the scale of this awesome town. Writing this gave me the perfect opportunity to have the best possible alpine experience. There is not a second when you are not skiing that you don't miss it.

So if you have not done so already, why not pay a visit to Chamonix and find out for yourself. If you have not tried skiing why not give it a go. Book yourself into a resort and make sure you take some lessons - what physical activity are you going to be doing on a regular basis when you get older? You are never too old to start skiing! What have you got to loose –

and hating the cold just isn't an excuse. Modern ski clothes will keep you warm even if you were in the Antarctic's worst blizzard. So "harden up" and give it a go!

As for my claim that Chamonix is the most famous ski resort in the world there is no doubt that this is true and this book is proof of that. However this accolade does by no means make it the best ski resort in the world. As I have mentioned, there is plenty of room for improvement. The infrastructure needs to be addressed, public transport improved and for god sake replace all those ancient ski lifts. I do hope the downhill skiing is held at Chamonix for the 2018 Olympics but there is plenty of work to be done.

So where is the best ski resort in the world you may ask? To me it's a simple answer, its wherever you are skiing with friends or loved ones. I have had many of the best and most memorable days of my life on skis whether it was learning at Lake Ohau ski-field, with friends and family at Coronet Peak field in Queenstown, long winter seasons skiing the on the active volcano at Mount Ruapehu and of course discovering European ski-fields and Chamonix.

As for me, I've come away from the mountains feeling fitter, stronger, healthier and happier than I ever thought possible when I arrived. My broken heart is healed and whilst my financial problems haven't gone away my renewed zest for life means I that am now taking responsibility for them.

Chamonix helped rekindle my inner joy and the hope of new possibilities, renewing a darkened spirit and igniting courage. I know that whatever I do next will be with the same passion that I've invested in my skiing, my friendships and my book. I have the satisfaction and contentment of understanding now that the solutions to the rest of life will follow!

Thank you Chamonix Mont Blanc, the world's most famous ski resort.

"Winter sports do not belong to those which one is content to watch; it is necessary to take part. No summer sport is their equal in a perfect and healthy pleasure. It cannot be analysed: it is an abundance of joy, movement, exaltation and health. It is the death of neurosis and dark thoughts; it is the ruin of the doctors, it is the crash of patient medicines; it is strength, it is a flowering, it is happiness".
Gerard de Beauregard 1908

LaVergne, TN USA
19 January 2011
213149LV00002B/59/P